Endorsements

The fruit of a godly legacy is a life lived with empowered faith, and no one embodies that more than Tom Grassano. We grew up together in the same church youth group, and his dad, Pastor Thomas Grassano, was my pastor. So, I am not surprised at the legacy that is continuing through this anointed family. Written with such care and truth, I know *Walk with Me* will inspire, bless and encourage you to believe God for all that He has called you to do in this very important season we are living in. Nothing is impossible when a life truly surrenders to God as my friend Tom has done. Read and be inspired.

Joni Lamb, Daystar Television Network

Dr. Tom Grassano has been a special friend and prayer partner for years. I have seen him personally as he ministered to the hurting people of the South Bronx. I have heard his voice and his heart as he has cried out to God for the anointing required to fulfill his assignment. I love his wife Lidia, and I am so proud of his daughter, Angel and son, Tommy. This is a family who shares a calling and a mission for God.

Walk with Me tells the story of transformation and offers a message of hope, love, and benevolence, inspiring the reader to take leaps of faith where there has been hesitation. This story, with personal struggles, presents a challenge to each of us to love unconditionally, to treat people with dignity and respect, to meet people where they are, and to rest in the provision of God.

Walk with Me will challenge the reader to discover that fulfilling God's plan is not always easy, but it brings immense joy. When God is glorified, the world becomes a better place.

Dr. Raymond Culpepper, International Overseer, Church of God

Tom Grassano is a gifted writer, orator and musician. He also happens to be one of the most intelligent, passionate and committed men I've ever known, in any walk of life. Along with his wife, Lidia, and their children Angel and Tommy, the Grassano family has taken their unshakeable faith from the roughest, toughest neighborhoods in America to some of the most remote regions the world to carry out their one unifying mission – bringing hope on behalf of our Lord and Savior, Jesus Christ!

I have been amazed, inspired and deeply humbled as a personal witness to the way in which they have answered their calling. May God continue lift them up and bless them, always.

Trevor Thompson, Fox Sports Detroit

I met Tom and Lidia Grassano for the first time in 1988 and became immediately aware of their passionate vision for the harvest. I personally witnessed the effectiveness of the entire Grassano family and their ministry when I visited them in the South Bronx. I knew that day that Tom accepting the call to plant and pastor a church in the Bronx became the Lord's commission to embrace a much larger and life changing purpose.

It is all too easy to become insulated from the community in which we are called to serve as the cares and burdens of life and ministry demand our attention. Outreach is essential in the call of God to today's world. Tom Grassano's proven effectiveness through years of ministry make this book a must-read for anyone desiring to combine the burdens of outreach and local ministry. Tom brings alive the concepts with which he has been divinely gifted over a lifetime. These gifts, combined with relationships, experience, and passion, have resulted in transformation and effective ministry.

Dr. Tim Hill, International Overseer, Church of God

The calling of God to a person is one that is as beautiful as a rose, but the thorns of life cause us to remember that our service is for the Creator of the rose. Dr. Grassano's life and passion is one that needs to be told. It is a story which will inspire the most insignificant person to become the most significant person in a world that needs to hear how the love of God transformed them.

Felipe Martinez, Executive Assistant to Mayors Bing, Cochran and Kilpatrick, Detroit, Michigan

Dr. Grassano is a humble servant of the Lord who has done whatever it takes to bring Christ's life and love to the hurting of some of the neediest communities of our nation. Despite many threats on his life, difficulty and little financial backing, he and his family persevered and have discipled and trained many who have now become part of the answer. This is a story that must be told!

Rev. Nick Savoca, Director of Prayerstations.org

I have known Dr. Tom Grassano his entire life, having had the opportunity to work with his father in ministry. Tom had numerous opportunities to become well established in church administration, teaching, and many other ministry options. Early on in his life, he made the choice to devote his life to planting seeds of hope in the hearts of the poor, and he has never given up on that dream.

Perhaps the thing that I appreciate most about Tom is that he did not try to establish and operate his ministry from a distance. He and his family have spent most of their lives among those to whom they are ministering. I know of no one who has greater compassion for and greater expertise in ministering to the disenfranchised that exist in the urban community. This is a story worth reading.

Dr. R. Lamar Vest, Former President/CEO, American Bible Society

Dr. Tom Grassano is passionate about taking the gospel of Jesus Christ to the "hard places" in our world. Under Tom's leadership, Urban Harvest Ministries is being mightily used of God to transform lives and neighborhoods, and his vision and passion is a catalyst that is causing many others to want to be part of transformative ministry.

Tom has shared his message, his ministry, and his passion with our students here at North Greenville University, and God has used him in a powerful way to challenge and mobilize our campus to take the good news of Jesus Christ to the nations. His love for the Lord is obvious, his story is compelling, and his spirit is contagious. I highly recommend my friend, Tom Grassano, and his story to anyone that has a genuine heartbeat to making a difference for Jesus Christ.

Dr. Allen McWhite, Executive Director of the Institute for Global Leadership, North Greenville University

Dr. Tom Grassano is the real thing when it comes to integrating faith into a life of sacrificial service. I have been privileged to know Tom since his college days. His seriousness of purpose is undergirded with a genuine joy embracing a love for the Lord and for all of God's children.

In a time when many ministers are striving for personal attention, Tom's constant focus is on increasing the love of God and neighbor among all, especially for those living in the shadows of poverty. Tom's ministry is not about "look at me," but directing our vision to the impact of urban decay on brothers and sisters in need of help and hope, and a faith that redeems and reconciles.

Dr. Tom Grassano's constancy of commitment over the past thirty years has made and continues to make a life transforming difference in the lives of many. He truly represents one of Furman University's finest!

Dr. Jim Pitts, Author and former chaplain, Furman University

WALK with ME

Bringing the Hope of Jesus

No Matter the Cost

By

Tom Grassano

*All scripture references are from the Holy Bible,
New Living Translation © 2015 by Tyndale House Foundation,
unless otherwise noted.*

ISBN: 978-1-64288-143-1

Printed by Derek Press
Cleveland, Tennessee

To my children, Angel and Tommy,

Carry the torch for all to see.

"Fan into flames the spiritual gift God gave you…"

2 Timothy 1:6

Two roads diverged in a wood, and I –

I took the one less traveled by,

And that has made all the difference.

From *The Road Less Taken*
by Robert Frost

"Those who are wise will take all this to heart;

they will see in our history the faithful love

of the LORD."

Psalm 107:43

Expressions of Gratitude

To Mom and Dad: The effects of your prayers and your example continue to go with me and my family, and they always will. You are an inspiration and guiding light to me. I am deeply grateful to God for you, my parents. I am humbled and honored to carry on your legacy of faith and serving God in complete abandon.

To my wife, Lidia: This journey would have been impossible without you. Thank you for being my partner in ministry and in life, my faithful companion and best friend. I love you immensely.

To Angel and Tommy: Watching both of you grow into the young woman and young man that you are has brought more joy to me than any other thing I have experienced in my life. To see you now serving and loving people and honoring God answers not only our prayers but the prayers of your grandparents as well. Being your dad has made me the proudest man on earth. I am proud of you. I love you both.

To those who have journeyed with us from our Harvest family: Maurice, Vonetta and Joanne, Raul and Vilma, Cathy, Peck, Sharon, Allie and Dre, Willie and Shami, Karl, Gina, Christian and family, Les and Mikael, Nathan and Mikey, Keith and Marie, "Tiny" and so many others, you are loved immensely. I thank God for each of you and the important role you have had and continue to have in the vision of Harvest.

To Spike, Craze, Sonny, Chino and Yamira, Joseph, Victor, Mito, Roz, DJ, Rosie, Manny, "Gordo," Maria and many others of my Brook Avenue family: Thank you for the honor of being a part of your lives. I love you all and continue to pray for you.

To our *Hope for the City* family: What an honor to serve with you! Thank you for your prayers, your partnership, and the ways that you continue to serve your city.

To Phuc, Trinh and family, Hien and family, Buu, Thuan, and all our very dear friends in Vietnam: I am blessed and honored to know you. You shine the light of Christ. God smiles when He sees you.

To the many men who have been important influences in my life, past and present: Floyd McClung Jr., David Wilkerson, Raymond Culpepper, Robert Fisher, José Minay, Ray H. Hughes, John Nichols, Tom Wieland, Nick Savoca, Wayne Merritt, Lamont Freeman, Roger Helle and Lamar Vest - Thank you for your love, your example, your prayers, and for believing in me and my calling.

To "Race Pilot" Bill, Dwayne, "Big Rev," Vera, Jim and Bekki, Bill and Judy, Trevor T., Tim and Dusty, Mike and Toni, "Bistro" Bill, Angelo, Art, Sherry, Larry W., Rich and Shirley, Julie and Ben, Erwin and Joyce, Helen, Les and the Rincon family, John and Patsy, and our many faithful Partners in Ministry: *None* of this story would have been possible without your prayers and support.

To Peck Sim, Rick and Kailee Isham, and Douglas LeRoy: Thank you for your editing expertise. And to Andre Morton, the most gifted graphic artist I know: Thank you for allowing God to use your artistic talent on the cover of this book.

To Robbie Vorhaus: This book would have never been completed without your encouragement, words of wisdom, inspiration and occasional "push." Thank you for the gift of your friendship which I cherish ever so greatly.

To my Heavenly Father: You saw in me what others did not. You gave me a purpose greater than myself. You never gave up on me. I am eternally humbled and thankful for Your love and the honor and joy to walk with You.

Table of Contents

Foreword

By Robbie Vorhaus

I am a Jew, the son of a holocaust survivor, a 5th generation New Yorker from Manhattan. I was physically forced from my home and left homeless for several months at the age of 17. These and other events led me to surrender my life to Jesus Christ, declaring Him my Lord and Savior. My job is advising global leaders, celebrities, politicians, and sports stars on successfully navigating life crises. I believe that all these points of distinction make me uniquely qualified, and honored, to write the Foreword to Dr. Tom Grassano's new book, *Walk with Me*.

Dr. Grassano and I met almost twenty years ago in Beaver Creek, Colorado, at The Renaissance Weekend, a prestigious, invite-only retreat for global leaders working in media, religion, the arts, science, technology, medicine, business, and finance. Here at 8,000 feet above sea level, on this glorious late summer day, stood this tall, good-looking man with dark hair who had a striking resemblance to Elvis Presley. Walking among the rich, famous, powerful, and notable, with an air of someone who knew a secret he couldn't wait to share, Dr. Grassano, armed with the eternal truth of the Bible, carried himself with the confidence of invulnerability, and to anyone who would listen, shared his message of love, compassion, the benevolence of service, and most importantly, hope. And listen they did. When Tom Grassano talked about the power of Jesus Christ and his ministry, everyone in attendance -- truly everyone, including staff, support, service people, non-Christians, and agnostics alike -- stopped in their tracks and listened with rapt interest to his incredible stories of God saving lives and souls on the dark and dangerous streets of the South Bronx.

Again, please recall, I am a New Yorker. There are several truths native New Yorkers know: bagels and cream cheese count as a meal; the Empire State Building and the Brooklyn Bridge remain iconic landmarks; walking is the best form of transportation; the best free outing is a round-trip ride on The Staten Island Ferry; there's nothing more beautiful than the Rockefeller Center tree at Christmastime; and if you value your life, there are simply certain neighborhoods you avoid. So, it should have come as no surprise that a few years ago, T (as I call him) invited me to witness his ministry in, at the time, the arguably most dangerous, drug and rat-infested, poverty-ridden, lawless part of New York City, the neighborhood known as Fort Apache in the South Bronx.

So notorious and ruthless was Fort Apache, that Paul Newman starred in the 1981 film by the same name about a beaten-down New York City cop who, after witnessing one horrific act after the other, tried unsuccessfully to bring a sense of law and order to his police precinct and neighborhood. So here I was, after taking a long subway trip north and filled with dread, that I found T with his big smile and strong gait, walking the streets of Fort Apache with no fear, greeting and stopping to talk with residents who obviously were thrilled to see him. It was as though T was surrounded by light, pulling everyone in his path into his compassionate warmth as he seamlessly and without effort shared the hope of Jesus Christ with residents of a neighborhood many would say God forgot. But not Tom Grassano.

For the next two decades, T and I became friends and colleagues. Overlooking my gruff and sometimes inappropriate amount of cursing, over the course of me writing my best-selling book on happiness, *One Less. One More.*, T was my spiritual advisor. When a client, friend, family member, or someone in the media wanted Christian counsel, I reached out to T first. And when I needed to hear the embodiment of Jesus Christ in human form, it was him I called.

Every great story is about a character's journey through an extraordinary world and how, over the course of time, lives are changed forever, and the world looks different because our hero comes to town. Tom Grassano courageously lives a life filled with passion, authority, and danger, all in his service to a loving God who can change lives for those who choose to listen and follow. His story is, to its core, an exciting and suspenseful tale of love, persistence, promise, and hope.

I promise, this book is for you. How do I know that? Because in my work with leaders, celebrities, sports stars, government and church officials, and others, everyone to the person is fighting some battle and needs to know in their heart-of-hearts that, with Jesus, they are never, ever, alone.

Walk with Me is a message of hope. It is evidence that God is alive, that, if we allow Him, He will be actively engaged in our lives. *Walk with Me* offers undeniable proof that hope in Christ turns emptiness into opportunity.

Even before you finish this book, you will be made better, filled with more love, greet your days with more expectation, and be in greater service to Jesus Christ, all by knowing this magnificent book, *Walk with Me*.

After 20 years, witnessing Dr. Tom Grassano in action has been nothing short of a miracle, which is assuredly what you will experience when you read *Walk with Me. Bringing the Hope of Jesus No Matter the Cost.*

Robbie Vorhaus
Austin, Texas
December 2020

Introduction

"You are the salt of the earth."

Matthew 5:13

Have you ever considered salt? Humor me for a moment. Take a saltshaker in your hand. An imaginary one is fine. Shake some salt into your palm. Now taste it. What does it taste like? Salt, of course!

Now shake a little more salt into your palm. What does it taste like now? Did adding more salt change the flavor?

Let's do it again. Shake some more salt into your palm. Do it liberally. Taste it. What does it taste like now? Did more salt change the flavor this time?

We all know the answer to this "semi-scientific" experiment: *We can put salt on salt all day long and it will not change its flavor.*

If salt is not made to put on salt, what then do we put salt on?

I have asked this question to many people. The common answer is food. I ask people to go deeper than that. What does all food have in common, whether it is from the land, sea or air, when we put salt on it?

It's all dead. It has no life.

At least I hope you're not chasing your chicken around the chicken coup trying to put salt on it or salting your fish while it's still flopping around in the pan.

Jesus said we are the salt of the earth (Matthew 5:13). If the purpose and function of salt is not to be sprinkled on salt, then why do we spend the majority of our time, our planning, and our budgets in our churches and ministries trying to figure out newfangled ways to put salt on what's already salty? Why are we so focused on those who have *already heard* rather than those who have *not yet heard?*

Why is our focus trained so lavishly on those who *already have hope*, rather than on those who *have no hope?*

This has been one of the greatest discoveries of my life, and I saw it among one of the greatest tragedies I have ever seen in the Fort Apache community of the South Bronx. This community of death, hopelessness, fear and despair saw Jesus as a figure on a cross and a person from history, but His love and hope wasn't alive in their world. His peace was distant and out of their grasp. They did not know God loved them when He formed them in their mothers' wombs and that He ordained a destiny for each of them before they were born (Jeremiah 1:5). They did not know He has plans for them that are good (Jeremiah 29:11-13). They did not know they could *touch* Him, and He would *embrace them*. They did not know how loved and special they were to the God who created them. Fear and pain had gotten in the way of those truths, and no one was walking among them with the hope and peace that could change their destinies.

God showed me more. I saw the same in the abandoned streets of Detroit. I saw it in the faces of people in Cuba. I saw it in the most decrepit and rejected favelas of Sao Paolo. I saw it in the slums of Guatemala and the mountain villages of Southeast Asia. They do not know. They have not heard. The words of God in Isaiah 6:8 compel me, *"Whom shall I send? Who will go for us?"*

I read the poem *The Road Less Taken* by Robert Frost in my 11th grade American Literature class. It stuck with me, especially the last words of the poem:

Two roads diverged in a wood, and I – I took the one less traveled by, And that has made all the difference.

If I were to write *The Road Less Taken* for my own life, it would be something like this:

I came upon two roads. One led down a familiar path that many had trodden, following man's plans, conforming vision to already-established methods, and depending on personal ability for success.

The other led down an uncharted, arduous road that would break me into pieces, make me totally dependent on God, and lead me to those who are desperate for hope. In the process, He would show me how truly real the Jesus of scripture is today.

And *that* has made all the difference in my life.

I thought I had my life figured out: teach in a university, lead a campus ministry and serve somewhere in missions in the summers. I had done that for years. I married a missionary's daughter, and we did it together. It was an exciting life. When I completed my doctorate, I knelt in my office at the university, held that parchment up to God and said, "My life is Yours! Do with me as You desire."

Jesus responded, *"Walk with Me."*

From that moment, God would begin to weave my life into a journey from the concert stage and the classroom to the streets of the South Bronx, and from there to the nations. He did not ask me to walk behind Him. Walking behind Him doesn't invite as much participation and partnership. He did not want me to walk in front of Him. When I did get ahead of myself, He lovingly, and sometimes sternly, brought me back. He invited me to walk *with* Him, *beside* Him, into a journey of discovery of who He is and of His very present power to relieve suffering and to bring hope and life to everyone, everywhere He would send me.

Accompany Me down the road I have designed for you. Walk beside Me so that you can see what I see on this road, and so that you can see people the ways that I do. Don't worry that you do not know tomorrow; I do, and I will take you there. I will teach you along the journey. We will be salty together. I will always be with you. Walk with Me.

People today don't need impersonal arguments about the Gospel message, as true as those arguments may be. What people need is Jesus with skin on. They need Jesus to walk their streets in our feet and enter their world with His love and hope alive in our hearts. They need to know that He will do for them what He did for the blind beggar on the roadside, the crooked businessman in a Sycamore tree, and the prostitute who had sold her soul so many times she didn't know who she was anymore.

The salt of eternal hope yearns to fulfill its purpose. It longs to spring forth from us. Just like a candle should not be placed under a bushel but placed on a table to light the entire room (Matthew 5:15), so our salt must get out of the saltshaker and be sprinkled on the world around us. It is our purpose on this earth. It is our destiny.

Jesus called me to walk with Him in the midst of suffering, neglect, rejection, brokenness, fear and human pain, to help others discover Him and the destiny He divinely and uniquely designed for every person on this earth. His calling was never about what I would do; it was about what He could do and I could not: transforming lives eternally with His hope, healing people with His love, destroying fear and despair with His truth, and setting lost and hurting souls on the path to destiny.

This is a story of walking with Jesus. This walk has included suffering, pain, death threats, cold winters with no heat, living on limited support, opposition of witchcraft and the organized church, sickness and death. I came to the end of myself over and over and always found Jesus there, waiting, with a fresh portion of His presence for that valley and the next part of the journey. This walk broke me, challenged me, and changed me. Most important of all, people far more broken than I were healed and transformed by the grace of Almighty God.

Jesus wants to walk into the places where hope departed a long time ago. He wants to walk to the doors of the broken and empty wherever they are. He longs to be present where there is desperation, hopelessness and pain. He calls you and I to walk there with Him.

I learned something truly spectacular walking with Jesus: when I say yes to follow Him where and how He chooses, wounded, hopeless, and neglected people begin to live again.

Chapter One

"Follow Me"

"No eye has seen, no ear has heard, and no mind has ever imagined what God has prepared for those who love Him."

1 Corinthians 2:9

"You've been here before. I remember you!"

I didn't anticipate hearing those words during my first trip to the South Bronx. It was in May of 1992. I was leading a three-week outreach in New York City with college students, something I had done previously in many cities and nations. We had already spent two weeks in Flatbush (Brooklyn), Jamaica (Queens), Spanish Harlem, Washington Heights and other areas of New York City. We had experienced amazing things, but I never expected what I would encounter that day in the South Bronx.

Delayed by traffic, we arrived about 30 minutes late to a drug and alcohol rehab center called *"The Way Out."* This organization had been ministering effectively in the South Bronx for many years, led by a godly woman who began with a compassionate act of faith bringing homeless addicts into her home. It was our purpose to encourage the residents and have a worship service with drama, music, testimonies and sharing together in God's Word.

The residents were thrilled to see us. It was apparent that they did not have many visitors from outside of New York.

During joyful greetings and hugs, Cathy, one of my students and mission team members, brought one of the men to me. He was about my height, standing a couple inches over six feet tall and with a healthy handshake. With a look of wonder and amazement on her face, Cathy said, "Doc, you've got to hear this guy!"

The man joyfully said, "I'm Hector. You've been here before. I remember you!"

"No," I responded, "This is our first time in this part of the Bronx, but it's great to meet you!"

"No, you've been here before. I remember you."

He kept insisting, so much so that I was reminded of the old TV commercial about your brain on drugs with the eggs cooking in the fry pan. *How could he remember me in a city of millions of people when we come only three or four times a year?*

He insisted even more. "I remember you. You were here about this time last year."

Well, he was correct in that observation. We were here with a team of students in May of 1991, our first outreach in New York, but we did not come to this section of the Bronx. Just coincidence? Maybe. But then his words grabbed my attention in a life- changing way:

"You were in New York City in May of last year and you were wearing those same T-shirts. I remember you!"

He was right! We were in New York City in May of the previous year and we were wearing the same T-shirts with a cityscape of New York City and the words *Jesus Died for you!* But "How could he remember us?" I thought. "What in the world is this guy talking about?"

He continued. "You came to me when I was living in the Times Square subway station. You talked with me and prayed for me. If it wasn't for that, I wouldn't be here right now."

Speechless. It's rare to find me totally speechless, but at that moment, I was.

I stood in wonder and amazement at the providential footsteps that God had led us through. In a moment, I felt as if God wrote these words in the clouds with His finger above Hector's head:

"So will My word be which goes forth from My mouth;
It will not return to Me empty,
without accomplishing what I desire,
and without succeeding in the matter for which I sent it."
(Isaiah 55:11 NIV)

Hector and I talked for quite some time. I remembered him sitting behind a construction barricade in the Times Square Subway Station near the stairs for the platform for the N and R Trains. He was frail, unkept and totally dependent on crack cocaine. He said he weighed about 135 pounds and had not eaten or bathed in weeks. It was the last night of that outreach trip to New York City, at the end of the day. We thought we were finished with "ministry" and we were on our way to a late dinner before preparing to depart the city, but ministry never ceases if our eyes are opened to the world around us.

Now Hector stood before me healthy and in the middle of a dynamic life change. I was amazed at the providence of God, and His infinite grace in revealing Himself to us in that profound manner. What an awesome God.

Hector graduated from *The Way Out.* We kept in touch for a few years. He was reunited with his wife and children in Elizabeth, New Jersey. He started his own business – a carpentry shop. He called it *New Creations.* A very fitting business for a guy remade by The Carpenter.

We returned the next day to the South Bronx. After spending more time with Hector and the other residents at *The Way Out,* I took two of my students on a prayerwalk down Brook Avenue. We wanted to know the community and to understand how to reach out and how to pray effectively. Several from the rehab begged us not to go. We went anyway and learned the reason for their concerns.

Brook Avenue in 1992 was like a movie. Drug dealers controlled the streets. In a three-block section, the one-way avenue had two-way traffic as dealers sold their drugs almost like an assembly line to people in cars with license plates from New York, New Jersey and Connecticut. Crack was as cheap as you could get anywhere. Drugs and guns were visible. There was no need to hide them. One man was selling from a card table on the sidewalk. Not a policeman was to be found. Charges of corruption in the precinct were so prevalent that a police presence was not always a good thing to have around anyway.

Out of nowhere on the corner of People's Park, a dealer appeared. He walked right up to me and stood six inches from my face, his right hand inside his coat holding what could have ended my life that day. With intense hatred, he just stared me in the eyes.

There was no flinch in his rage-filled face.

I said a quick prayer. I still remember the words: "God, if anything happens right now, just take care of Lidia and Angel, and may You be glorified." After what seemed like eternity but was only a moment longer, he walked away and yelled down the block, "White band, bajando!" In essence, he announced to the other dealers, "White guys coming down the street!"

God was with us and I was grateful. But the environment of the South Bronx and the fear and despair on the faces of people were almost overpowering. Hope had been absent here for a very, *very* long time. Survival seemed to be the sole priority in the minds of residents. Children had no childhoods, being robbed of innocence through exposure to things no child, or even adult for that matter, should experience. Drugs and violence ruled the streets. Death was an evil and all too present companion.

This was Fort Apache, the South Bronx. No wonder they called it "Vietnam."

St. Mary's Park, potentially a beautiful park in the community, was off limits after dark to anyone who was sane. No one in their right mind would go through the park; the dangers were too great. Most playgrounds were empty. In the ones that were not, mothers or grandmothers kept a look out for anything and everything that could harm their children. Many times, young children as young as four years old played in the playgrounds without supervision and were left to fend for themselves on the streets. Were their mothers working? High? Stoned? Too young to know what to do with a child? In a way, it didn't matter. The child was still alone in a dangerous park at a very young age.

Coming to work in New York City with these annual outreaches, I mistakenly assumed that, with the intensity of needs around them, the churches in New York would surely be reaching out with relevant methods to bring change and empower the poor. But in most instances, this was not the case. Out of inward focus, lack of training, fear, or a weird combination of those, churches kept ministry in their four walls where it was at least somewhat "safe." Church was a sanctuary for the saints, not an empowerment center for changing a community. Fear in the body of Christ was so great that one church in the South Bronx posted armed guards on the roof as people came in and out of service. The result? The Gospel was irrelevant and impotent to bring change. The transforming power of God, relatively unknown.

But not to us.

We focused on the courtyard of the Betances Housing Projects, one of the largest housing projects in the area. East 146th Street between Brook Avenue and St. Ann's Avenue was made into a pedestrian street. It was a perfect place for outreach, except for its notoriety for violence and gangs. We were strongly counseled not to go there. "Too dangerous for a bunch of 'white' outsiders," we were told. We would be very visible targets. To me, this was why we came. *Light shines brightest in the darkest places,* so that is where we went.

We brought puppets, mime, clowns, basketballs, games, music, and contrite hearts driven by love and worship of the only One who could change this place. We played, laughed, and listened to people's stories with increasingly broken hearts. We prayed for them, encouraged them with eternal Truth and continually pointed to Jesus. The responses of people to a kind of love they had never experienced were beautiful and inspiring, lighting up the faces of children and adults with a glimmer of hope, if only for a moment, before the reality of their lives smacked them in the face yet again.

After seeing our genuineness and lack of ulterior motives, even teenagers and gang members responded. Having known him for only three days, one gang leader whispered to me in a park, "I want out, but I don't know how." We were moved by the openness of their hearts and their desperation for something *authentic*, something *true*, that they could hold on to through the storm and help them reach out for a destiny that up to that point had completely eluded them.

We knew the answer was in the cross, and we made sure not to present a socio- cultural representation of the gospel from the Bible-belt or any other culture. The naked cross was enough - no gimmicks, tricks, slogans, pat-answers or anything else. Strip away all that is not the reality of the cross and present the bare-naked truth to broken people. That's why Christ came. That's why He sent us here.

Developing a genuine relationship with us could open their hearts to a genuine relationship with Him. That's how Urban Harvest began and that's what it still is today: Building relationships that lead to salvation, discipleship, and the empowerment of people toward their destinies. That brings Him glory, and that changes communities *one person and one family at a time.*

A new friend, David, had controlled drugs on Brook Avenue in the past. After ten years in the penitentiary and another two years in the faith-based rehab *The Way Out*, his life had changed. He was now working at *The Way Out* and in a local church on Brook

Avenue. Our friendship and partnership in ministry quickly grew. He named Lidia and I the godparents of his new son.

I wanted to buy a greeting card and put a gift in it for David's family. I saw a store called "One Stop" on Brook Avenue just around the corner from the rehab. The store window was filled with merchandise and the sign on the outside of the store read, "Stationary, Gifts, Supplies and Other Varieties." Foolishly, I thought I could find stationary, gifts and supplies in that store.

The store was a drug front that only sold "other varieties." I didn't know that until I walked in the store. I looked at the man inside smoking a blunt (a marijuana cigar) behind a Plexiglas and wood barricade and asked the only thing I could think of:

"Do you have greetings cards here?"

I have thought about that and laughed many times since. The look he gave me was more of a "You idiot" than a look of anger. He shook his head saying "No." I said "Thanks" and walked out the door.

I found out later that day that someone walked into the same store two weeks prior, asked the wrong question, and was shot in the head. They dumped his body on the sidewalk of Brook Avenue, an avenue well accustomed to the stain of blood.

As I walked out of the door of this little store front on Brook Avenue, I looked atthe abandoned casket factory across the street. It was huge, occupying half of that New York City block. Abandoned for 30 years and in complete disrepair, it was now used by drug dealers and homeless drug addicts. Gangsters would dump bodies there and hang a stuffed animal on a tree on the corner to instill fear in the community and to announce, "Keep out of our business." The five-story abandoned building was a daunting figure in the community, avoided by anyone except those who had "business" there.

Walking out of that "One Stop" store and looking at that abandoned coffin factory, the Lord surprised me with compelling words spoken almost audibly to my heart:

"Prepare yourself, Tom; I have future ministry for you here." I knew at that moment that I would never be the same.

Chapter Two

Preparations

"I know the plans I have for you."

Jeremiah 29:11

"Prepare yourself" came to mean many things to me. Prepare my heart. Prepare my family. Develop greater insight to the city through research, formal study and on-site experience. I visited cities and walked the streets of inner-city communities like Overtown and Liberty City in Miami, Techwood and Capital Homes in Atlanta, the South Side of Chicago, Savannah, Boston, New Orleans and, of course, the boroughs of New York City. I interviewed and observed those doing ministry in these cities. I searched the scriptures for principles that would guide us in the unique urban ministry God was calling us to do.

But God had His own ideas about preparing me. Break my pride. Crucify my flesh. Kill the dreams that were mine and not His. Remove people from my life. Bring new influences into my life. Have His Spirit make me pliable enough for God to use. That painful process is exactly what He beckoned me into.

The mission organization with which I ministered had grown under my leadership from 187 participants the first year I was there to over 2,000. Teams of many varieties were commissioned into service around the world: first timers, evangelism teams, medical teams, construction teams, intercessory/missionary support teams, family teams, college expeditions. We prepared the short-term missionaries with four-and-a-half months of pre-training focused on their hearts, making them pliable enough to be used by God in effective ways and leave a testimony of the fragrance of Christ. We followed up the experience with six months of training and mentoring, fanning the flame to encourage serving others for the long-term. We provided training for the host sites, establishing prayer initiatives and helping format a ministry trip that would complement and facilitate the long-term vision of the host site rather than being an interruption.

We were driven by a desire for good stewardship of the time, resources and people involved in the short-term mission experience. We sought to do all we could to ensure the experience was not a "passing ship in the night" but transformational for all involved, producing fruit that would remain.

I visited New York City every two months and made sure to walk the streets of the South Bronx every time I visited. The more I walked these streets, I found the need for united efforts that would bring change and especially for relevant and effective strategies of outreach. The needs of the inner city would never be met without developing partnerships. Churches would never walk into their role as change agents in a community without vision for community transformation and without leaders empowered to follow that vision and make it a reality. The streets would never be changed without relevant, strategic methods of outreach and someone to take the initiative to engage in those methods, to walk alongside the people and serve them in the process. None of it would ever succeed without being bathed in love and prayer.

We returned to New York City in May of 1993 with another nearly month-long mission. We developed close partnerships with local churches and began preparing them for relevant ministry among the urban poor while leading them by example. We brought college and seminary students. With exception of those who had been with us before, they had no experience in urban ministry. I remember one student who said she had a 20-mile drive from her house to the closest McDonald's. Another said he had two traffic lights in his hometown: one was necessary and the other was there so the first one would not be lonely. We quickly learned that where they were from was not important. Who they were becoming in Christ and how we prepared them for the mission at hand was what really mattered.

We taught these students about faithfulness in little things: humility, a teachable spirit, serving others, developing friendship with God and other aspects of the crucified life. The result was a team of people who were pliable in the hands of God, Spirit-led, hungry for Jesus to demonstrate His glory, and focused on mission with compassion for people.

We met many people on the streets with desperate needs and saw God's hand intervene. We went into the dark places that many others didn't want to go, walking the streets of Spanish Harlem, Washington Heights, Flatbush (Brooklyn), Jamaica (Queens), and the South Bronx. We built rapport with the drug dealers and gangs, developing mutual respect that God would use later for His purposes.

We walked into parks and playgrounds controlled by drug dealers and began to play with the children, shoot hoops with the teens (often the dealers and gangmembers themselves), and through these things, built trust and relationships. We always took our daughter with us. People would question us about bringing a child one, two, and three years old into such places, but God used her presence to open the hearts of mothers to my wife and to show the people we were genuine about our work and our relationships. This spoke loudly to the people:

We do not think of ourselves as too good for our child to associate with you. We enjoy our little daughter playing in your parks and playgrounds with your children.

This was a powerful statement to the people. After all, God called us as a family. He brought us there as a family. He would use us as a family, and He would protect us.

We brought the pure presence and love of Christ into communities without reservation and with passion for their healing, hope and peace. God opened doors just because we answered His call to *be there.* We learned that we could accomplish much by simply being present with the love of Christ.

This was precisely what God did in a park off Bronxwood Avenue in the Bronx. It was adjacent to a junior high school and controlled by gangs. We did not know that at the time we went. Some of our team of college students began to play with the children. Some shot basketball with the guys and our girls hung out with the teenage girls that were there. At the appropriate time (always dictated by the Holy Spirit tugging our hearts), we offered to do some drama skits for our new friends. Mixing comedy with the expressions of the truth of scripture, God touched their hearts and they loved it. We could see the impact in their eyes and on their faces.

We returned a second day and a third day to deepen the relationships. I was able to befriend the leader of a gang. As we sat talking on a park bench, he turned his face to me and away from his "crew" and said, "I want out. I don't know how." I poured my heart out to him as much as I could while still being discreet. I prayed for that seed to produce fruit that would remain.

We invited all of them to our drama presentation at a nearby church that night. To our surprise, seven young men and four young women came. We ministered with drama, mime, music and testimonies, and then I gave a short, relevant word about destiny and hope in Jesus Christ.

When we opened the opportunity for them to begin a new life in Christ, the tension rose. Three of the girls stood and attempted to leave their seats and come forward, but the girl on the end of the row pushed her knees against the top of the pew refusing to allow her friends – girlfriends of the gang members and drug dealers – to move past.

On the other side of the aisle, as all seven of the young men rose to respond, two young men came barging into the church and stood in the middle of the aisle – just in front of their peers – challenging me. It was the gang lord and an "associate."

I was encouraged as the pastor rose from his seat on the platform, thinking he was going to provide some support. Instead, he walked away, moving to the back portion of the sanctuary. In my flesh, I said, "Well, thanks for the help!" Then I noticed as he stopped at the back wall and silently began to cry out to God with his hands raised in fervent prayer. I did not feel so alone.

God mercifully gave the words. I began to speak directly to who they were and what the needs of their lives really were. I challenged the gang lord standing in the aisle in front of me with the Truth, praying intensely in my spirit. I knew if he did not move, none of the others would, no matter how much they wanted to respond.

Suddenly, I noticed that the gang leader became uncomfortable, shifting his weight from one foot to another, looking down at the floor rather than staring directly in my eyes. God's Spirit was speaking to him, not me:

"You lay awake in your bed every night, staring at a dark ceiling, wondering if anything will ever change, thinking about those that have gone before you, wondering how soon you will be in a grave or locked up like them. Feeling the pain of the empty hole in your heart. As much as you have tried to fill it, nothing will. It hurts. You are surrounded by people, and you are still so alone. *God has better!* He has an ordained purpose *just for you. You* ***do*** *have a reason on this earth, but it's not doing what you are doing now.* You can change. You do not have to be afraid."

I looked the gang leader in the eyes and said, "You can begin today, not just for yourself, but for all of these. You can lead the way."

The shifting of his weight became even more intense. His hands were fidgeting in his pockets. His shoulders began to sway. Then, he picked up one foot, moved it back and forth a bit, and finally in complete release, stepped towards me. All the others followed him to the altar and gave their lives to Christ that night.

We promised them we would meet them in the park the next day. We did. To our pleasant surprise, they were in church on Sunday. We left them in the hands of that church and saturated them with prayer.

Later that week, we were scheduled to do outreach in the Jamaica Queens Market. Delayed by traffic, we arrived later than planned. As we began setting up for a Gospel drama presentation, a lady from a store came out and said, "You're lucky you weren't here 30 minutes ago! A guy was stabbed right where you're standing!" God was in charge of the time, even when we were concerned about the delay.

We did drama that drew the attention of the crowd, connecting with the people with humor and Truth. We performed a mime called *"The Redemption Mime"* that portrayed the Creation, Fall of Man, and Redemption of Christ. As we finished, Butch, one of our team members, read from Isaiah 53 and spoke about Christ.

Suddenly, three Nation of Islam adherents jumped in front of the crowd. (The Nation of Islam is an African American derivative of Islam founded in Detroit). One of them began challenging Butch with a question, "What color was Jesus' skin?" Butch attempted an answer pointing back to the story of salvation, but this man would not listen. He was Satan's agent to steal the Truth that God was planting in people's hearts. He became louder and angrier as he spoke.

Then another team member. Eloy (a godly young man from Ecuador) jumped in front of everyone. With the authority of Christ and His Word, Eloy spoke in a loud voice for all to hear, "The color of His skin doesn't matter! What matters is the color of His blood!

What color was His blood? It was red, and it was poured out for you and me!"

At that very moment, Satan's plans were crushed, his agents silenced, and the power of the Truth rang forth. Many opened their hearts to either receive Christ as Savior or to call out to Him for the personal needs in their lives as we prayed with each of them.

"What was meant for evil, God made for good, for the salvation of many ..."(Genesis 50:20).

We realized God was doing many things at once. People were hearing the Gospel. Places of spiritual darkness were being penetrated with hope. Christians were encouraged that fellow Christ-followers were spreading the light of the gospel in their communities. God's people were being challenged about living out the Great Commission. We became passionate about preparing God's people for relevant and effective ministry, especially among urban youth.

Toward the latter part of our month of outreach in New York in May of 1993, we spent a full week in the South Bronx, centered on the Betances housing projects. The projects were notorious for drugs, gangs, and violence. It was a place everyone was told to "stay away," but those were the very places we felt compelled to go. *"How can they hear about Him unless someone tells them?"* (Romans 10:14). Someone had to go. Why not us?

The people were starved for hope. More than 70 people made professions of faith that week. The openness of people to the gospel was exhilarating and frightening at the same time. We rejoiced that people were turning to Christ to change their lives, but we were also asking ourselves, "Who will disciple these people when we are gone?" We were planting the seeds of hope in good soil, but without a resident ministry in their immediate community to nurture the seed, would it bear fruit that remains as God desires?

God had a plan. The very same friend who made us the godparents of his newborn child felt called by God to plant an English-speaking church in the area. This was vital. Although there were Spanish-speaking churches in the community, both the presence of legalism and the usage of the Spanish language were deterring young people from going to church. David understood the community and the testimony of his changed life from the drugs and violence of the streets was well-known.

As a result of our outreaches, David's first service had over 60 congregants. After some were weeded out, David was left with about 30 people to begin discipling and empowering them toward their destinies. We continued to keep in touch with David and his family and did all we could to encourage them in this process. Until something unforeseen happened.

David's congregation had been worshipping in his home church, literally across the street from the projects where we centered our ministry in the South Bronx. He had been using his home church on evenings when there were no other services. Things were going wonderfully. The witness of Christ with grace and unconditional love was pouring into this community, until the senior pastor approached David and informed him that he saw no benefit to have this English-speaking outreach in his church. Furthermore, the people coming did not fit the "clientele" that he or his people desired. The work was shut down. David eventually moved to Brooklyn and began reaching people there through bi-lingual ministry. We were back to the same question: *Who will disciple these precious people and empower them toward their destinies?*

We continued working in the community, visiting several times over the next year to reach out and love the people. God was deepening our relationships and through that God was growing the respect and confidence the people had in us. Each time, it was harder and harder to leave because of our love for them and being more and more touched by God's heart for them.

God began revealing His plan. As part of a seminary class on Urban Missiology, I wrote a paper on a theology of urban missions, focusing on methods of community transformation. It centered on networking suburban and urban Christians in Great Commission partnerships, establishing prayer initiatives, empowering leaders in relevant and relational ministry, leading in strategic outreach, and sharing ownership with local leaders of the vision for community transformation. I titled the paper *The Urban Harvest.* This would become the foundation of our mission.

While prayerfully seeking God's guidance, three people came into my life with the same question: Floyd McClung of Youth With a Mission (who became a mentor and personal prayer partner for several years), Bob Pace of Men of Action, and Daniel Ramos, a youth minister from Chile. None of them knew each other, yet each one had the same thing to say. Their question became a message from God to me.

"Tom, if you could do anything with nothing holding you back, including finances, what would you do?"

"I would move to New York City and begin an outreach in the South Bronx."

Upon hearing the answer, each of them quoted the same scripture: *"For God is at work in you, willing and working for His own pleasure"* (Philippians 2:13).

Sitting in my office in February of 1994, I told God, "Many great things have been accomplished with this mission organization. It is on a path to continued growth and impact. You made me a person willing and eager to accept a challenge. I no longer feel the challenge here. What do you want me to do, Lord?"

Shortly after, God allowed a series of events that shook our foundations and drove us into a much deeper reliance on Him. With my closest prayer partners and mentors, we began to feel, "It's time." Two spiritual leaders with whom God had given me close relationships – Ray H. Hughes and John Nichols – agreed.

But not all agreed. Many stood in opposition to the vision. Others didn't agree with the timing of it. Still others just looked at this as a crazy idea. They wrote us off and removed us from their radar. Some, in good intention probably concerned for our safety or where they thought we should focus our ministry, tried to point us in other directions, even presenting lucrative opportunities elsewhere.

Sometimes you just know. Sometimes that feeling is so deep in your heart it becomes a part of you. You can't escape it. The thoughts are with you day and night. The vision is so real you can almost see it as reality before it takes place.

There are always risks in following the voice of God. We can be misunderstood. We can lose the favor and fellowship of those who think we should go in another direction. We can be wrong. The only way to truly know is to launch.

It was time for a giant leap of faith.

Chapter Three

You Chart the Path Ahead of Me

"You chart the path ahead of me."

Psalm 139:3

We made the decision to move to New York City. My wife Lidia and I packed and prepared for the journey with our four-year-old daughter, Angel. As I finished packing my office, I took down the poster I had made with the words of Steve Camp's song, *Run to the Battle – "Some people want to live within the sounds of chapel bells, but I want to run a mission a yard from the gates of hell."* It was time to live the words of the song I loved.

Our vision was to empower leaders, lead in outreach and establish initiatives that bring world changing followers of Christ out of the church buildings and into the streets. We had laid the groundwork to begin the fulfillment of this vision over the four previous summers of outreach in New York City, three of which focused on the Mott Haven community of the South Bronx. Churches of many cultures across Brooklyn, Queens, the Bronx and Manhattan were requesting our partnership and were thirsty to be empowered to reach effectively into their communities. Even before moving, our calendar was booked for six months across New York City to begin training church leaders and leading in outreach.

We followed by faith as God enrolled us into His intensive seminary. He would use many heartaches and challenges, successes and failures through which the process of refinement and simplification of approach would continue years after we began our work in the Bronx. I studied theology before I moved to New York, but God trained me in urban ministry in the seminary of the streets of Fort Apache, the South Bronx.

Our sending agency had committed to provide some needed foundations for us to begin the work. One of those was housing. They had sent us keys to a small house owned by the agency located over an hour from the Bronx in the center of Long Island. With my dad's VW Golf pulled behind a Ryder truck, we drove to New York and finally arrived at the house. It was in a modest neighborhood, but it looked more than sufficient for us.

Until we opened the door.

The previous resident had not completely moved out and the house was in complete disrepair. Railings on the stairway were broken. Tile had fallen off the bathroom walls. Walls and ceilings were damaged. A metal pipe duct-taped to a 2x4 for support provided a place to hang clothes in the master bedroom closet. The kitchen consisted of four walls with two pipes sticking out of one. We were forced to quickly formulate a back-up plan by putting our stuff in storage and living in a room in a ministry office. After spending two months in that office, we moved into the house, sleeping on the floor and cooking with a toaster oven and microwave while we sat on the living room floor. We memorized the menus from the take-out Chinese restaurant and pizza place a block away.

We raised money to repair the place after being informed by the ministry organization that was the only way repairs would take place. We bought closet systems, carpet, and blinds. We repaired walls and doors with holes in them. We fixed the broken plumbing in the bathrooms. We repaired leaks and painted. When some neighbors placed their 25-year-old kitchen cabinets on the street for the garbage to pick up, we asked for them, purchased a countertop and a sink, and after several months without one, finally had a kitchen. Upon installation of the sink and countertop, I stood at the counter turning the faucet on and off, saying "Thank you, Lord" repeatedly. I never knew I could be so happy with a kitchen sink!

We were grateful for all these things. It began to feel like home. Then, about a week after the repairs were finished, the leader of the ministry agency invited us to a Christmas dinner and informed us they were selling the house and we had to move.

Merry Christmas.

At the same time as those things were taking place, my daughter became ill. She was four years old when we moved to NYC and had never really had any health problems other than the seasonal cold. The very month we arrived in New York, Angel began to have respiratory problems and severe allergic reactions. Her throat would close. She would break out into a severe rash. Her face would swell. We were in and out of doctors' offices and emergency rooms, and the medical insurance we were promised never came.

Then, we were informed that our start-up funding would come to an end.

Our God does not abandon His children, but it began to feel like it. *Had we missed God's call?*

Instead of abandonment, we would see the miracles that I had heard about as a child in my parent's lives. Lidia became ill. She postponed going to the doctor because of our lack of insurance and finances, but her health worsened, and I had to take her. We found a medical office and set an appointment. After the doctor treated her, I went to the window to pay. "It's taken care of today," the receptionist said. To this day, we don't know how. We knew no one there, and no one knew our situation, except our heavenly Father.

During our first year in New York City, a seamstress friend of my mother offered to make some clothes for Angel. The package finally came with the clothes and a bill for the material. We didn't have enough money to pay it. We looked at the clothes quickly and left for a service at a Haitian church in Brooklyn. After service, the pastor's wife (who spoke little English) called my wife into the pastor's office. She handed Lidia an envelope and said, "This is for Angel." Lidia opened it on the way home. It was what we needed to pay the bill for the clothes. There was no way she could have known about the need, and there was no way the timing could have been more precise - just like the stories of God's provision for my parents and grandparents. *"I have never seen the godly abandoned or their children begging for bread"* (Psalm 37:25). Jesus Christ is *"the same yesterday, today and forever"* (Hebrews 13:8). God is faithful.

Still, the trials combined with the opposition of someone we thought was a close family friend that was to partner with us caused me to really question. I did not question God. I questioned myself. Late one night after Lidia and Angel had gone to bed, I went downstairs to be alone with God. It was about 1:00 am. I laid on the smelly floor, crying out, *"God, I have missed your calling! I wanted to come to New York. This was my idea. I'm sorry! Get us out of here!"*

Then God spoke. Not with thunder and lightning flashes in the sky. In that "still, small voice" He said words that I will never forget:

"Be faithful. Be obedient. Persevere."

There were no promises of immediate breakthrough if I would. There was no time limit put on the present trials or "in six months, things will be better." Neither was there direction to do anything or expect anything differently. Just *"Be faithful. Be obedient. Persevere."*

But He spoke. I had to listen and trust that somehow, somewhere there would be the grace to walk forward another day.

Shortly after this, I was invited to visit a church in Philadelphia that was interested to have me as their pastor. I never really saw myself in that context, but the timing called for our serious attention. The church wanted to be engaged in the inner city and wanted us to consider taking its leadership. I never would have thought of Philly before. *"God, did you get me to New York to go to Philly?"* I began to think that was the case.

Two days before we left to visit the church in Philly, I received a strange phone message. The message was from David Wilkerson and he wanted to speak with me. I thought it was a joke, for I had never attempted to speak with him. I held David Wilkerson in the highest esteem. I had read many of his books, and I had visited Times Square Church on 51st and Broadway, which he founded and remains a powerful lighthouse in the city of New York. For those who remember, the book and movie *The Cross and the Switchblade* tells the story of his journey from rural Pennsylvania to the streets of Brooklyn.

I heard Pastor Dave speak when I was 13 years old. God spoke to me that night and it impacted my life. I never forgot it. I never thought I would meet him.

The day before leaving for Philly, I called the number in the message. It was Pastor Dave's personal assistant. I apologized for bothering her and remarked that someone might be pulling my leg. She said, "No, Pastor Dave wants to speak with you." In a moment, I was on the phone with David Wilkerson. He spoke a few words, asked a few questions, and invited me to his office the next Tuesday.

Lidia and I left the next morning for Philadelphia. It was a nice church located just a block from the Trolley that could take you straight to Center City. We saw the surrounding area. If I were to pastor, it seemed it would be a nice place.

"But is this what You want, God?"

Sunday morning came and we went to church. The people were kind and greeted us with warmth.

"But is this really what You want, God?"

The service went well. We met with the leaders after the service. I had a lump in my belly. All afternoon I was uncomfortable and kept asking, *"Is this really what You want, God?!"*

We arrived back at the church for a service in the evening. As the musicians and singers led worship, the Lord spoke so boldly to my heart that it felt like Jesus walked right in front of my face:

"Now that I have your attention, go back to the South Bronx. Plant a church and raise up an outreach center. Reach out to children and through that, reach their families. Establish households of faith that will be lighthouses in that community. Empower people toward the destinies I personally designed for each one of them."

I spoke on my vision that night, but it wasn't the vision the people in Philly expected to hear. I don't know if my wife expected to hear it, either. I spoke about the South Bronx and the needs. I shared about our experiences and I shared my understanding of God's plans for us in South Bronx.

No other words were needed after the service. "Nice to meet you" was good enough. We all knew I was not the future pastor for that parish.

But I did have a future in the South Bronx. I had understood my calling to be that vision I wrote about in that seminary paper *The Urban Harvest*, a vision empowering leaders, leading in outreach, establishing prayer initiatives, and building networks for sustainability. That was why I went to New York City. We had already laid the foundation and the responses were more than I anticipated with churches constantly contacting me and my calendar filling up five to six days a week. The need, and the thirst, for training in relevant outreach and discipleship was greater than I even expected.

God had me lay down that vision that was so precious to me. That which I had spent three years formulating, studying and researching to develop. That which pastors and church leaders were so desperate for. That which was beginning to produce fruit and experience success.

I felt like I was laying down my ministry as Abraham was called to sacrifice Isaac, but I didn't know if I would ever pick it up again. Pastor Dave shared about it once. He called it *The Death of a Vision.* I heard that sermon series at Times Square Church the first few months I was in New York, going through these challenges. Something in my gut said, *"This is for you!"* but I refused to accept it, until I had no other choice.

Death is painful when it is close to your heart. Death of a vision is scary because it leaves you feeling as if you are teetering on a fence unsure of which way to fall and scared to fall at all. In those situations, we must fall into God's grace and into His hands and believe He is faithful to lead us.

We returned to New York on Monday and I was in Pastor Dave's office on Tuesday. I didn't know what to expect, had no idea how to prepare, and had no clue how the conversation would go. I went over and over in my mind what I would say when given the opportunity. Each time I thought of it again, it would change. I finally settled on just being transparent about our situation and what I was trying to understand about the Lord's ways in our lives at that time.

Pastor Dave came out of his office, introduced himself (like I didn't know who he was), shook my hand and invited me into his office. He asked a few questions, and in so doing I realized that, without me saying anything, he completely understood our situation. God Himself had revealed it to him. Then he said, "Tom, let's pray."

We prayed for one hour and fifteen minutes.

When we finished, Pastor Dave gave me five books: *Hungry for More of Jesus* which he authored; *The School of Christ* by T. Austin Sparks, and the three-volume set *The Christian in Complete Armour* written in 1655 by William Gurnall and reprinted by World Challenge. Then Pastor Dave said, "Let's meet again in two weeks," and we said goodbye.

I spent the next two weeks continuing to seek the Lord's direction while somewhat bewildered over my encounter with Pastor Dave. One thing was for sure: He gave me these books; I felt I better read them.

During those two weeks, I began to hear more rumblings of opposition, mocking and demeaning the path we had chosen. The words sometimes came with false accusations and bitter lies. The injury was heightened when I realized the source was a family friend, a man whom my father had mentored. He now had authority in the ministry supposedly supporting our efforts in New York. One of his board members, a man whom I also considered a friend, asked me to lunch at a diner for what I thought was fellowship. Instead, it was his time to vent his anger over the things he had heard and to levy accusation.

My blood boiled as I sat listening. I formulated my responses and was ready to give ample proof of how he had been misled and deceived. Then the Lord spoke to my heart clearly and directly, but not what I wanted to hear:

"Tom, would you please shut your mouth and let Me fight this battle?"

I was used to fighting battles. The young maverick in me fueled by my Italian blood was ready to boldly defend myself and set the record straight. The words *"Tom, would you please shut your mouth and let Me fight this battle this time?"* came as a shock and didn't sit well inside of me. But I knew they were God's words, and I knew that, while in my flesh I may be able to oppose certain men, I cannot oppose God, not without great consequence.

The man stopped spewing his accusations and waited for my response. I responded with calm and confidence. "I did not do nor say any of the things you have mentioned, but I will leave it at that."

He responded angrily, "Aren't you going to defend yourself?"

"No, the Lord is my Defender, and He will treat me justly."

About a year later, another minister visited this man's church. Somewhere in his simple sermon, he stated that he had just visited the South Bronx with Tom Grassano and saw the work that had begun. At the conclusion of his message, the pastor who accused me in the diner ran to the altar and wept openly. He then repented before his church. When I heard about it, I was reminded that God really is our defender. His ways are best, and He really will treat us justly if we trust in Him and walk before Him with a pure heart.

I returned to David Wilkerson's office in two weeks as he requested. I was nervous because I had read only two of the books he had given me – the first two volumes of *The Christian in Complete Armour,* each about 300-pages long. But Pastor Dave was not interested in book reviews. He was interested in my heart, my family, and God's calling on our lives.

"How have you been the past two weeks? How are Lidia and Angel?" We spoke for several minutes about these things.

Then he asked the question of questions: "Tom, what is God telling you about your ministry?"

"Pastor Dave, I believe God is telling us to go to the South Bronx to plant a church and raise up an outreach ministry there. To reach children and through that, reach their families. To establish households of faith that will be lighthouses in that community and empower people toward their destinies."

Pastor Dave then asked, "What part of the South Bronx?"

"Mott Haven," I responded.

"What part of Mott Haven?"

I informed him of the area where God had called us.

Pastor Dave responded, "That's the heart of Fort Apache!"

You know how you sense something is about to happen? You feel in your gut that God is about to reveal a reason and a purpose for what you have been walking through? I had that feeling.

Pastor Dave astounded me with his next words: "I've been praying for four years for God to bring someone to that community!"

He continued: "Tom, if this is what God is telling you to do, Times Square Church will stand with you. We will pray for you. We will support you in this ministry. We will send workers there to help you, and you and I will meet to share and pray."

I had felt alone. I was deeply discouraged. We had no funds. We were losing our place to live. People – even so-called friends – were opposing us. My daughter was sick. I felt the calling of God to the South Bronx but did not see any means to walk into it.

But it was God's voice on the street three years before: *"Prepare yourself, Tom. I have future ministry for you here."* And now, God was making a way for it to happen.

A relationship began with Times Square Church that day in David Wilkerson's office that lasted for years. They prayed for us. Once I dropped off some materials in the office as the pastoral staff was leaving a meeting. They looked at me and said, "We just prayed for you!" Friends visited Times Square Church and called me afterwards, saying Pastor Wilkerson had called each of our family member's names in prayer in the service. They faithfully supported our family and the work. They sent workers to assist in various projects. They even encouraged their members who lived near us to come to our fellowship.

The most valuable of their investments were the one-on-one times I had with Pastor Dave. We would talk about ministry, about family, about family in ministry, about the city, about evangelism and about reaching people. We would talk about the uniqueness of ministry in an inner-city community like the South Bronx. He would share his experiences and wisdom with me. We talked about theology and about loving people.

He always asked about our family, and every time we were together, we prayed.

Everything that Pastor Dave shared with me regarding our ministry proved to be true: "Don't expect to establish a church like this. You are establishing a spiritual hospital, a place where many will come, be healed, and go their ways. You will never know what happens to most of them until heaven."

Nick Savoca, a man who had worked diligently in New York City for over 30 years and who used to work with Wilkerson's ministry met with Pastor Dave after I did one day. (Nick, the New York Metro YWAM Director and North American Cities Director, became a vital prayer warrior and source of Godly wisdom for us to this day.) As Nick left Pastor Dave's office, he called me and said, "Tom, I learned today that you remind Pastor Dave of himself in his early days of ministry." I have had few things touch me more deeply.

The last time I met with Pastor Dave personally in his office, he did something a bit out of the ordinary. We would always pray after we shared and discussed ministry and the things of God together. This time , Pastor Dave said, "Tom, would you pray for me?"

I felt like an ant before a giant. *"Me? Pray for David Wilkerson?"*

To the best of my ability, I prayed for Pastor Dave, his family, his staff and the church. I thanked God from my heart for all they had done for us and the work in the South Bronx. We then prayed for the Bronx, for New York City, and for Christ to be exalted among the nations. We prayed for our families.

When we finished, Pastor Dave asked me to wait and stepped out of his office.

After several minutes, he came back in and stuck an envelope in my pocket. "This is not for the ministry," he said. "It is for your family, for Christmas. Buy something for Lidia and Angel." He wrapped his arms around me, embracing me. Then he looked into my eyes and said, "My office door is always open to you. I love you, Tom."

"I love you so much, Pastor Dave." I will never forget that day.

A vital lesson emerged from these early experiences. I realized how important it is to have a godly covering whenever we launch out to do anything for God. The prayers and counsel of those who have walked the path before us are of immeasurable value and must be sought after and cherished. Those relationships don't often come by man's appointment into titled positions. They come through God's divine appointment. They are fostered through prayer and transparency, and they provide an umbrella of protection over us as we walk by faith into the plans that God has laid before us. They have certainly been a strength to me. I cherish them and continue to seek them out today.

Angel suffered for 15 months with allergic reactions for which the doctors never found the source. Before Thanksgiving of 1995, I sent a simple letter to about 100 people sharing this need in my daughter's health and asking for prayer. Eight days after the letter was sent, Angel woke up able to breathe without any difficulty. The respiratory and allergy problems never returned.

And God would continue to be with us every step of the way.

Postscript: I received a message while studying in my office some years ago. I immediately went on-line to check the news, and to my dismay, the message I received was correct. Pastor David Wilkerson was killed in a head-on collision with a truck. A man of integrity, of passion for God's Word, of uprightness and intimacy with God and full of the Holy Spirit had left this earth. I honor the life he lived unto the Lord. I thank God for his legacy and his fingerprint in my life and the lives of so many. May God help us to follow faithfully in the footsteps of such great soldiers of the cross.

Chapter Four

Small Beginnings

"Do not despise these small beginnings, for for the Lord rejoices to see the work begin."

Zechariah 4:10

We had a lot of faith and a lot of vision launching out in the Bronx, along with a very deep compassion and burden for the people. We saw their lives destroyed, families broken, and too many people with no hope for the future. We wanted to instill into them a belief that there was something better, and they could find it in Jesus Christ.

Many years later, about 16 years after beginning the work in the South Bronx, I sat down with one of the former drug dealers and his wife. *Former* is a particularly important word, for it does not matter who they are, what they do or what condition they are in when they come. What matters is who Jesus created them to be. This *former* drug dealer has been working a good job for several years, raising his children and now doting over his grandson.

We sat down together and spoke about family, about losing his mother, and reminiscing about days gone by. I then asked him, "Why did you accept us? You could have fought against us, but you didn't. Why did you open your arms and accept us the way you did?"

"We didn't have a choice," he replied.

"I don't understand. What do you mean?" I asked.

"We didn't have a choice. You set up shop on our block and wouldn't leave."

Setting up shop. Those words made a lot of sense 16 years later, but God had to do a lot to help us "not leave."

I had a meeting with Pastor Dave Wilkerson the Thursday before we launched the ministry. It did not go as I had anticipated. I prayed ahead of time and put together some questions to ask him in this final step of faith for our next steps in the Bronx. I began by asking, "Pastor Dave, what is your final advice to us as we launch in the South Bronx this weekend?"

He turned and looked out the window of his office overlooking Broadway and Times Square, mulling over thoughts in his mind for what seemed like an eternity as I waited with anxious anticipation. Then he turned his face toward me, looked in my eyes and said, "Jump in the deep end and learn how to swim."

What?! I was so disappointed. I thought to myself, "All of his experience, his wisdom, his depth in Christ, *and this is what he tells me?!"* I realized years later how profound and Spirit-directed his words were. God's plan for me, for us, was not to enter this work with understanding and clarity, but to enter with our eyes fixed on Jesus and to learn all that He would teach us about reaching hurting souls in the inner city. After many years of education, completing my doctorate and then starting seminary, the streets of the South Bronx and the people who call them home would become the most important classroom in which God would teach us how to love and empower those whom He loves and wants to call His own.

The people God called us to reach lived in a community referred to as "Vietnam." Devastation made its home here in many ways. Our community was the poorest Congressional district in the U.S. The average combined annual family income when we arrived was slightly over $11,000. Asthma was eight-times the national average. Tuberculosis and other diseases were prevalent. Still today, 25 percent of expectant mothers are HIV Positive. Forty-seven percent of grandparents raise their grandchildren, largely because of AIDS and drug addiction.

Over two-thirds of elementary school students fail reading proficiency tests for their grade. In four of the six Junior High Schools in NYC School District 7, less than 10 percent of eighth graders passed these tests. In one school, only 1.2 percent passed.

High school dropout rates range from 50-80 percent. Sociologist Jonathan Kozol (author of *Amazing Grace* and *Ordinary Resurrections)* stated that, of 1,000 freshmen in a South Bronx high school, half are repeaters, only 90 will make it to 12th grade, and about 65 of them will graduate.[1] This is precisely what we have observed over the years in the South Bronx.

Our precinct was one of the most violent in NYC and in the nation. Drugs ran the streets and ruined countless families. Twenty-five percent of children went hungry every day. The most devastating statistic of all was that over 85 percent of children were fatherless. Sociologist Jonathan Kozol observed that "Mott Haven is among the poorest and deeply segregated areas of the country and suffers from an epidemic of asthma [eight times the national average], AIDS, father absence and homelessness. It is a neighborhood where even the cats and dogs die young." [2]

Poverty was present not just economically but morally and spiritually. For many years, our community led the nation in rape and incest per capita. Three forms of religion were prevalent: Roman Catholicism, legalistic Protestantism, and Santeria. The strict form of Catholicism was like that which my wife and I had encountered in Latin America, unaccepting of anything that was not its own form of faith. Many parents in this tradition would pull their children out of our after-school tutoring and mentoring programs, preferring them to be on the streets without help than in our doors. The Caribbean Latino Protestant churches were rooted in legalism. The list of rules was long and harsh, and applied more to women than men - long dresses, don't cut your hair, no make-up, no pants, men's hair can't touch their collars, no facial hair but thick mustaches allowed, no movies, no beaches, no love, no hope, no joy. But lots of noise. The volume of their worship services was loud, but their witness was voiceless and silent. Youth in the community were not attending the Catholic churches, and only those forced to attend by strict parents were still in the Protestant ones.

The third form of religion in our community was Santeria. Santeria is a mixture of Catholicism and spiritism, or demon worship, a tradition very prominent among the Puerto Rican and Dominican peoples. Santeria shops are all around our community. We often found signs of rituals where chickens had been killed and the blood used in sacrifices, or cow's tongues nailed to a tree. Once, for 16 straight months, every time we arrived at our outreach center, we had to clean up the remains of Santeria rituals performed on our doorsteps as witchcraft spells were being conjured against us.

Jump in the deep end and learn how to swim. Translation: Be obedient to your call and lean hard on God with an open heart and a teachable spirit while you set up shop.

We needed a place to begin our work. I contacted David, a transformed young man who had run part of Brook Avenue and had a reputation in the community. God had changed his life, but people still knew the old David and respected him.

David said he had just the place for us to begin our work. He asked me to meet him at "The Way Out" drug and alcohol rehab where I had met Hector almost three years before. I thought we would jump in my car and drive somewhere. Instead, we walked around the corner to a chapel in what previously was a meat market. It was part of another rehab ministry on Brook Avenue. It was, by God's providence, right beside the store front I had walked into over three years before, across the street from the abandoned casket factory. There I was, standing on the same side of the street and same sidewalk where I had heard God say, *"Prepare yourself, Tom, I have future ministry for you here."*

Three years before, I thought "here" meant New York City. I was wrong. Here meant right here in Mott Haven. Right here on Brook Avenue and East 148th Street. *Right here on this block.*

We made a verbal agreement to rent the chapel for two hours on Wednesdays and three hours on Saturday afternoons. Wednesday would be a discussion group/Bible study/counseling session. Saturday would be our children's outreach. Five months later, we would have our first Sunday service.

We were thankful to be familiar to the community. During our frequent trips to the Bronx for over three years, we had walked the streets, reached out to children and youth, and conducted block parties and community concerts. Our first outreach was an outdoor rally in the courtyard of the Betances Housing Projects on East 146th Street in May 1992. We had returned many times. The people knew our faces. The children who attended our outreaches were happy to know we were back.

Acquiring a space would not change the focus of our ministry. We walked among the people, going to parks and playgrounds, meeting people on the streets, building relationships. Through this, a handful of people began to come on Wednesday nights. We sat in a circle and talked about their problems, about relationships, about their needs, putting these things into a Biblical perspective and pointing to Jesus. Since all the people we were reaching were unchurched, we had to begin with the most basic aspects of faith. As they began to place their faith in Christ, they began to experience some things they had never really experienced before, like joy, hope and peace. They would express it in the ways they knew how, using every form of profanity to describe how good Jesus is. The simplicity of their faith blessed me.

We did not begin in the Bronx with a marketing plan; we began building relationships based on the pure love of God. We did not begin with a large ministry team either. Our ministry team consisted of six: me, my wife, our four-year-old daughter, the Father, Son and Holy Spirit. God blessed us with two servant-hearted interns who would serve God with us for a short season. We did not have a building, a sound system, an office, a website, a vast mailing list, or any of the things considered normal and necessary today to launch a ministry. What we did have was a calling from God, a community with *enormous* needs, a heritage of trusting in God, and some people praying for us. To us, that seemed enough.

In God's divine providence and wisdom, He placed us in *the* building in our community. It was a notorious building where drugs ruled. Drug dealers had broken the locks on the mailboxes, changed the locks, and stashed their drugs in the boxes. The post office didn't even attempt to deliver mail. A couple of the apartments above were homes to influential drug dealers. They hustled in front of the building, at the corner store, and across the street in the abandoned casket factory.

It was January of 1995 when we began our Saturday children's outreach and Wednesday night discussion class on Brook Avenue. The statistics became reality. Poverty and suffering had faces and names that we now knew and loved. In the compassion of Christ, our hearts were broken. We learned very quickly why so many inner-city ministers either burn out or become calloused and cold: the enormity of the need and the weight of the burden were overwhelming. After two-and-a-half decades of doing this work, I still believe that, in this context, personally leaning on Jesus must be coupled with a strong marriage, accountability and prayer support to carry the burden and stand victorious in this intense field of spiritual warfare.

A couple of years before moving to New York City, I read a book by Fran Sciacca entitled *Generation at Risk*, a fascinating and well-written book walking through the generations after WWII into the 90s. Some words Sciacca wrote have stayed with me to this day, speaking of *"the connection which defines shared pain and challenges us with the question of whether we will become involved or merely intrigued, . . . committed to the idea of compassion, motivated by the need for compassion, but far removed from the reality of compassion, not unlike many of us who have become comfortable sending our "involvement" through the mail in the form of monthly checks, while maintaining a sort of sterilized distance from the reality of individual human pain"* (*Generation at Risk, page 109*).

The essence of the Parable of the Good Samaritan is in Sciacca's words. In reality, the parable is about the *Great* Samaritan. You and I are the ones who fell to the thief and were left for dead. Organized religion and tradition could not save us. Then the One *"despised and rejected, a man of sorrows acquainted with grief"* (Isaiah 53:3) saw and perceived our need. He came to us, pouring the oil – the washing of the Holy Spirit, and wine – His blood, on our wounds so that we could be healed and set free. He took us to an inn – the church - and left us in the hands of the Holy Spirit and His servants, and then said, *"When I return, I will repay you."* Then, in yet another form of the Great Commission, Jesus said, *"Go and do the same"* (Luke 10:37).

We met a family who lived in the casket factory in the dead of winter. The mom and dad were addicted to crack cocaine. The child lived a hopeless life with them. We loved them and pleaded with them to change, for their sakes and especially for the sake of their son. Rats ate two of the dad's toes as he was stoned on crack. The family eventually disappeared, and we never heard from them again.

Lidia led the children's outreach with the help of the two interns who lived with us. It focused on building relationships while having fun time and story time. We began with two children, our daughter Angel, and Andrew, the son of a young ministry couple who felt called to come from Long Island to the Bronx to serve.

We made some flyers and distributed them in the areas of the community where we were already known and accepted. Toward the end of January, a 9-year-old girl named Rosaline walked in and asked what was going on. Quite bold for her age, she was like so many other children in the community forced to grow up beyond their years because of what they experience on a daily basis, but too often robbed of the innocence of childhood at a very early age. Rosaline and her 12-year-old brother, Raymond, began attending the children's outreach. We met their mother, Maria, and began visiting them weekly in their home. Their home was a small apartment two blocks from the small chapel we rented. It was on the corner of East 149th Street and St. Ann's, on the second floor of a building over 100 years old and in complete disrepair. In this small, two-bedroom apartment, Raymond and Rosaline lived with their parents, their older sister and her baby, two Rottweilers, and an iguana in a large, homemade cage.

Maria didn't know who we were or what to think about us. She, like everyone else in the community, did not trust outsiders. They questioned my agenda and wondered who I really was. *"Is he a cop? A Fed? Who is this guy?"* I learned many years later that the entire community watched our every step during those early years. My wife being Hispanic from Chile fit in more than a 6'2" Italian American man. I was a spectacle. Raymond told me later that I was "the only white guy walking the streets of our community who wasn't a cop or a slumlord." Because of our consistent work with the children and the authentic love of Jesus they felt through us, Maria and others began to accept us. Thankfully, Maria - this woman who was not only Rosaline and Raymond's biological mother but the "mama" to the drug dealers in the community - eventually accepted Jesus Christ as her Savior, and Jesus broke her addiction to crack.

Maria's compassionate heart was bigger than her apartment. When her niece Crystal began to rebel and was kicked out of her home, Maria brought her in. When six-year-old Carlitos, born with AIDs from his parents' intravenous heroin addiction, was left without a home, Maria brought him in. Then Maria found Samuelito, a ten-year-old boy practically living on the street. He had been thrown out by his mother and was living with his heroin-addicted father who did nothing to care for him. Maria found Samuelito without shoes nor a coat in the dead of winter in the Bronx. All these children became part of our children's outreach.

We purchased a coat, shoes, school supplies and other things for Samuelito. The joy on his face was like a young child on Christmas morning opening the most special gift. Samuelito was so happy and so proud of the things that God had provided for him. Then his father sold them all to support his heroin addiction. We went shopping again, and Maria brought Samuelito into her home.

The reality of human pain. Children, at the fault of parents, experiencing far more than any child, or adult for that matter, ever should. Our hearts were crushed and broken again and again.

What did we have to give these people? All the ideas that I had brought to the Bronx began to crumble at my feet. Reality was more painful that I had imagined. There was no hope. A person can be without walls, without relationships, without doors of opportunity opening before her, yet still have hope and survive. Here and in many places like Fort Apache, the people had no hope. I realized that many of the ideas I had brought to the Bronx were not only irrelevant, but they had no power to change anything. The people here needed love in its purest, most authentic and unconditional form. Yes, they needed faith, but first they needed love. And they desperately needed hope.

1 Corinthians 13:13 never made more sense to me: *"Three things will last forever – faith, hope and love – and the greatest of these is love."*

---

[1] *Bearing Witness in the Twilight.* Newsweek. May 21, 2000

[2] *Bearing Witness in the Twilight.* Newsweek. May 21, 2000

Chapter Five

A Place Called Home

"I am going away to prepare a place for you..."

John 14:2

Speaking at a church in Atlanta in 1995, I gave a prayer request:

"We need a van and a building of our own. I don't care what condition they are in!"

Wow, does God answer prayers specifically sometimes.

A few weeks after that service, I received a call from an inner-city ministry in Atlanta. They had an old van they needed to get rid of and thought of us. I was thrilled. *It was free!*

I flew one of our interns to Atlanta to pick up the van. When he saw it, he called me and asked, "Are you sure you really want this?"

It couldn't be that bad, I thought.

I was wrong.

This 1978 Ford 150 11-passenger van had one seat in it, the driver's seat. A plastic Walmart chair was where the passenger seat had been. Stick shift on the column. No windows in the sides or rear. Dashboard charred from fire. Holes everywhere from rust, including one big enough in the driver's floorboard that I could stick the front of my foot through it. I called it my Flintstone van.

I truly had no idea what to do with this thing. That's when some godly men from Pennsylvania led by Erwin Bassler came to visit.

They took the van back to PA to work on it. Police stopped them on the way and inspected the van, wondering what kind of illegal activity was taking place. Once they heard the story, they had pity on the men and us.

God used these men to bring about a total transformation of this van. They found seats in a junk yard. They repaired all the areas of rust and had it painted. They installed a new transmission with a stick shift on the floor. They cut windows into the sides and back doors, and they installed ¼ inch steel in the floorboard. The thing was a tank! It was a symbol of what can happen when something looks like all hope is gone. These men truly did the impossible and gave us a symbol of transformation for our transportation.

We knew that God divinely placed us in the chapel on Brook Avenue and East 148th Street. We rented the chapel on Wednesday nights and Saturday afternoons. All the rest of our work was in the projects, in apartments, in the park and on the streets. After five months, we were able to rent the chapel an additional three hours on Sunday afternoon, having our first Sunday service there on May 28, 1995, which happened to be Pentecost Sunday.

We were thankful for the extra time on Sunday, even though we were sandwiched between two other church services. We would wait outside until the first service was finished, and then enter quickly to set up for worship. Having no windows, the swelter was almost unbearable in the summer months. It was a large open room with a small stage. Two bathrooms were in a tiny hallway on one side. We could only use one of the bathrooms because the floor of the other was falling through to the basement.

At times, leaders and members of other churches would come in during my teaching and interrupt, calling me a false prophet and telling our small group of people not to listen to me. They did this because, in their opinion, we "desecrated" their chapel by doing three things: drama ministry, puppet ministry for children, and not imposing a dress code. Legalism is deeply inbred in these churches.

You must look righteous in the ways they define before coming in their doors. If not, you are judged, harshly. We welcomed people however they were dressed and in whatever state they were, just like God does.

After establishing the after-school tutoring/mentoring program, we began using creative arts to teach life and scriptural principles. The students who were growing in their faith, committed to education and consistent in attendance were invited to become a part of a drama troupe. With a mix of God's favor, their amazing talent and relevant material (mostly original) that presented poignant life lessons, sometimes with humor, the troupe became quite popular. We often used drama on the streets, in parks and playgrounds, and in block parties. Over the years, we received many invitations to visit churches in New York City and eventually in other states in the Northeast, Mid-Atlantic and Southeast. We even fulfilled invitations to Mexico and Cuba. Working with these students was truly one of the greatest joys of my life.

The students chose the name *Exodus* for the drama troupe because, in their study bibles, Exodus was defined as "a journey out of bondage," and that was the journey they felt they were on. In the first year of *Exodus,* we were invited to perform in the church in our community where we had attempted to plant a church the year before moving to the Bronx. They had their annual youth convention and wanted our group to perform in a service. This was one of the first invitations in our immediate community and we were excited. We arrived early, checked out the stage, made sure the soundtracks were ready, and waited for the service to begin.

Shortly before the service began, I was called to the senior pastor's office. I shook his hand and thanked him for the invitation. Then he stated, "Your young people are not welcome here." I was startled. "Excuse me?" I asked. He stated again, "Your young people are not welcome here. They are not dressed appropriately."

I began to appeal to him. "These youth are poor. They are wearing the best pairs of jeans they own. And, Pastor, it is much more modest to do these dramas with pants than with a skirt."

His answer revealed the fear behind their legalistic rules. "If we allow your youth to minister in our service and God uses them, it will destroy everything we have taught our youth that God can't use people who dress these ways. But we would like you to remain and speak for our service."

What a confession. If God used our drama team, the lie of some of their legalistic doctrine would be exposed.

My response was simple. "If the sheep are not welcome, the shepherd is not welcome either." We returned to our ministry home and got on our knees to pray for that church and the youth that were there. We were not bitter or angry. Our hearts were broken.

This tragic story is an example of how these churches have become mirrored images of the Pharisees Jesus condemned, wearing their long tassels, gloating over their works, and having no love. It is no wonder that the very people who needed healing and hope most would not set foot in these churches. If they did, they would be judged by their appearance and not welcomed. They would not find love there.

I became acquainted with the pastor of the church that had service before us on Sundays. He was a good man with a sincere heart. He invited me to speak for his church service, which was a bold step for him. His elders had threatened to remove him as pastor if he didn't take a stand against the heretics from Harvest, referring to us, of course.

I invited two of our youth to come with me and do a drama skit. It was well- received. After the skit, I spoke from the parable of the Good Samaritan, focusing my teaching on the priest and the Levite. Upon conclusion, the pastor came forward and addressed the congregation:

"I prayed about this man. God told me He had sent him here and we should support what he is doing. That's why I invited him here today. After hearing this man speak, you now know that he is sent from God to our community. Many of you have criticized him and judged his work. God has now given you the opportunity to repent before this man of God."

Then he waited.

People from the congregation began to stand, starting with an elderly man I did not know, and ask my forgiveness for their criticism of us and our methods. They publicly asked me and God to forgive them, and they promised their prayers for us as we established our work in their community. This was a breakthrough and began a new relationship with that church as God moved them from judging us to wanting to learn from us.

Having an office in the back of our Volkswagen Golf and facility for only 10 hours a week, we became desperate for a place of our own. That was when a miracle happened.

It was Sunday evening, January 14, 1996. I was leaving the next evening for Vietnam. (More about that later.) We had just closed the chapel. As we walked to our car, I noticed activity at the old One Stop store. The Feds had shut down the store, but now they were taking off their locks and chains and returning it to the owner of the building. As we were leaving, the owner put up a "For Rent" sign.

I left for Vietnam the next day and was there almost three weeks. There were very few methods of international communication at that time. I made a brief phone call home my first day in Vietnam. It cost $30 and I heard someone listening in on the conversation. I sent messages home via carefully coded fax three times.

The storefront remained on my heart the entire time I was in Vietnam. When Lidia picked me up at JFK airport, the first thing I asked was, "Is the storefront still for rent?" Lidia responded, "Yes, it is, and I haven't been able to get it out of my mind either."

I acquired the phone number and called the landlord to inquire about the space. The owner's wife answered. She began asking questions about us and our work. One question led to another and then she said, "Is your ministry the one that Pastor David Wilkerson at Times Square Church prays for all the time?"

I informed her that it was.

She responded, "We go to Times Square Church! We have to rent to you! If we don't, God won't bless us!" Well, I didn't know about whether God would bless them or not, but I was silently fist pumping when I heard that!

Sue (the landlord's wife) then informed me that her husband Mike was on his way to the store to take the security deposit from an interested party. She got off the phone quickly to call him and give him my number. Shortly after, Mike called me, and we set up a time to meet.

Standing outside the store, Mike asked me how we fund our ministry. I shared with him about faithful people who donate to Urban Harvest. I also shared with him about the support from Times Square Church. When he realized the small amount that God was stretching for us to do this work, he said, "I won't take a penny over $300 a month from you, and I will throw in the basement for you to fix up for a youth center and clothing closet." This was less than half the rent. We shook hands and sealed the deal.

Urban Harvest now had a home in the South Bronx.

We lifted the gate and opened the door. This was my first time in this storefront since I walked into it in May 1992 and asked for a greeting card. At that time, there was a Plexiglas window and wooden dividers, but now the place was a mess. The dividers were toppled over, the barricade torn down, ceiling tiles and garbage all over the floor. A large refrigerator was toppled over, barely giving space to walk down the hallway to the back. There was a hole in the ceiling that I could not understand. The front room was about 11 feet wide and over 30 feet deep. A long and narrow hallway led to a bathroom and a 12x15 room in the back. The hallway was so narrow two people couldn't pass each other without one squeezing against the wall.

It would be quite an undertaking to clean out and renovate the space, which God knew before the miracle took place to lease it. Times Square Church responded with funding to help us buy the materials needed to renovate our first outreach center in the South Bronx. They also sent a licensed electrician to do the electrical work (which was quite entailed!). Our brother in Christ, Erwin Bassler, a contractor from Pennsylvania who was a leader of the construction ministry that renovated the van, came with some men from his church in Claysburg, PA. His team provided all the skilled labor. Three mission teams from Furman University (my alma mater), Lee University and Duke University came to serve on their Spring breaks. With Erwin's guidance, they put up paneling and sheetrock, spackled and painted, and cleaned out the basement.

We still had a hole in the ceiling. Erwin and I could not figure out what it was for. One of the drug dealers later approached me on the street. "Did you patch up the hole?" I learned from him that the hole was there to send drugs into the apartment above if the storefront was raided. He offered to seal up the hole and he kept his word. One day he walked in, asked for some tools and wood, and closed the hole. The drop ceiling was added, and we had our first home, *The Harvest Center.*

We dedicated *The Harvest Center* on Palm Sunday of 1996. The space was small but adequate. It felt like home from the first day. As soon as we opened, people would stop by to ask, "What is this place?" More children became involved in our programs as a result.

For the entire time we had been in the South Bronx, people kept asking us, "When are you leaving?" They were accustomed to us coming and going as we did the first three years of our involvement in the community. Now that we settled into our facility and word spread, people began to realize that we were there to stay.

We waited anxiously for better weather to come so that we could move ministry back outside. Having a home did not mean moving our ministry indoors. No, it was a base for outreach to the community. Here is where we did our planning, leadership development, discipleship, training for outreach, and tutoring when we began our after-school program. Everything else was outside, in the community, among the people.

On the anniversary of our first Sunday service, we moved everything onto the sidewalk, singing, sharing testimonies of changed lives, and celebrating the freedom, joy and forgiveness we had all found in Jesus Christ. It was a beautiful day, but for me, the day had much more significance. It was four years before that I walked out of that *One Stop* convenience store that was a drug front. As I stepped onto the sidewalk, I heard the nearly audible voice of the Lord speak to me, *"Prepare yourself, Tom; I have future ministry for you here."*

Now here I stood, on the same side of the street and on the same sidewalk where I heard God's call, in front of the old store now renovated to bring life into our community. I marveled at the divine purposes of God, planned in heaven ages before we even existed, guiding our footsteps into the plans that supernatural God had prepared for His children.

I think of what could have been. What if I had not listened? What if I had not followed His voice to the South Bronx? What lives would not be touched? What hope would not be brought to these hurting people?

On the way home one evening, I was talking with Jeff Wilson, a ministry student with an amazing servant heart doing a summer internship which turned into six years of working alongside us in ministry. We were excited about what God was doing and talking about the vision and dreams God had given us for the future. Then Jeff said,

"Just think about it! If we can imagine all of this, what does God really have in store! Ephesians 3:20 says that 'God is able to do exceedingly abundantly beyond all that we can ask or even imagine,' so what does God really have in store!"

What an amazing truth!

We learned very quickly in the South Bronx that while man's plans may fail, God's plans never do.

In July of 1995, we were ready for our first major outdoor ministry event of the year. This "block party" would incorporate games and fun for children and families. It would give us the opportunity to expose the ministry to the community and meet families so that we could identify their needs and respond. As has been our custom, at the right time, we would shut down games and fun and begin a time of sharing hope with the people in a relevant way.

We had only started the ministry in the South Bronx that January. Since we had no facility at that time, the courtyard of the projects and the apartments of drug dealers and drug addicts were our "sanctuaries." We defined church by Christ's words in Matthew 18:20, *"Where two or three are gathered in My name, I am there also…"*

We had planned this outreach event for months. A group of students from a Christian college came to do the music. I had worked with them before and I was impressed with the sincerity of their hearts. I knew they would be a good fit for the South Bronx. By God's favor, we were given permission to use the courtyard of the projects, even tapping into their power supply for the sound system. Many people came. The children played with us and parents expressed their appreciation for us coming to the projects. This was not common in 1995. God used this "spectacle" for His glory and to draw attention to His love for the community and His purposes for its people.

Though I was busy playing with children and talking with parents and teenagers, I was praying over the soon-approaching time of sharing hope and giving an opportunity for life change. I prayed for God to open the hearts of the people. As we were nearing the point to move into worship, clouds formed rapidly. Before we could even react, a downpour of rain began. As it continued, we realized that it would not stop anytime soon. At the most important time of the day when everything seemed so ripe to share the message of hope, we were forced to pack up the sound equipment and instruments so they would not be damaged in the rain and to close the event.

As soon as the equipment was secure, I separated myself and walked around in the downpour. The rain hid my tears over the deep disappointment I felt. I knew God was in control of all things, but I didn't understand why He would allow this to happen.

Many people had gathered. Their hearts seemed so open. Relationships were being formed. Everything was ready.

God was setting us up for the next year.

Fast forward to July 1996. We now have our own outreach center. Motivated by the vision of bringing hope to the streets, we scheduled a block party on our block - Brook Avenue between East 147th and East 148th Streets. We received a permit to close Brook Avenue and have the block party in the street in front of *The Harvest Center.* Like the year before but much larger, the event would include games, inflatables, face painting, balloon animals, music, drama and activities for all ages. This would give us the opportunity to meet families, identify their needs, and hopefully build relationships that would lead to empowering them toward their future. Mission teams from out-of- state were with us and people from around New York City were coming to enjoy the day with us. They would help facilitate games and interaction with people.

Everything was perfect.

Well, almost everything.

There was a 100 percent chance of rain. It rained the entire time we were setting up. Jeff ran to the store to buy more balloons for the water balloon toss (ironic, isn't it? Planning a water balloon toss in the rain?!) and came back soaking wet. "It's still raining?" I asked. Jeff responded with blind faith, "No, it's not!"

What Jeff, Lidia and I did not know was that each one of us was praying the very same prayer as we continued setting up the block party: "Lord, You stopped the sun for Joshua. You love us as much as You loved him. Stop the rain so that people can hear about You this day!" There just wasn't room in my heart for another day like the year before. This was the day the Lord had made. We wanted to rejoice and be glad in it.

The final preparations were made. The street was clean. The inflatables were in place. The games were ready. The sound system and instruments were inside the door of *The Harvest Center.* Mission team members were in place and ready. Some were out in the community to inform people the block party would still take place. Intercessors were walking the streets and praying. The rain had slowed to a drizzle.

Our permit stated that the block party would run from 1:00-7:00 pm. Promptly at 1:00 pm it stopped raining. The sun burst through the clouds and shined brightly on Brook Avenue. The block party began. Carnival games and inflatables were in full swing. We stopped every half hour to do group games – relays, tug-of-war, pie-eating contest, water balloon toss (which we needed now in the hot sun!). The group games broke the ice and forged relationships with people. The community began to see that we were not stuck-in-the-mud Christians, walking the streets with our long dresses, long sleeves and long faces with some judgmental, oppressive form of religion. No, we were relational. We were enjoyable. We were fun. Which meant that *God is relational, enjoyable and fun!*

People's hearts opened to us. As they did, their hearts opened to Him. Lives were changed that day, and for that all of heaven rejoiced. I rejoiced, too. At last year's block party, I had tears of disappointment. This year, they were tears of joy.

We later saw more of the significant impact that God made that day. Not only lives were changed, but our entire community saw that God cares. He loves them and He invites them into a lifestyle not of dark and gloomy religion, but as Jesus Himself said, *"I came so they can have real and eternal life, more and better life than they ever dreamed of"* (John 10:10 TMSG).

At 7:00 pm, we closed the block party. As we finished cleaning the street, it started to rain again.

The reports from people who came to the block party and from the evening local news revealed the reality of the miracle that day. For the entire day, it was raining all around us. Rain all day in Queens, Manhattan, Westchester County, New Jersey, Long Island, and even other parts of the Bronx. People who drove to the block party from those areas thought it would be closed down because it was raining their entire drive until they entered our community and "a hole opened up in the clouds." Weather reports on local news channels that evening talked about the rain that fell consistently throughout New York City and surrounding areas that day.

But not on Brook Avenue in Mott Haven.

God had a purpose, and His purposes cannot be thwarted, even by nature. When He wants His Word to go forth, it will.

"For as the heavens are higher than the earth, so are My ways higher than your ways, and My thoughts higher than your thoughts. The rain and snow come down from the heavens and stay on the ground to water the earth. They cause the grain to grow, producing seed for the farmer and bread for the hungry. It is the same with My word. I send it out, and it always produces fruit. It will accomplish all I want it to, and it will prosper everywhere I send it. (Isaiah 55:9-11).

Chapter Six

Beauty from Ashes

"He will give a crown of beauty for ashes ..."

Isaiah 61:3

At nine years old, Robbie had already attempted suicide twice. He once set himself on fire. Another time he hung himself from his bunk bed with a belt tightly wrapped around his neck. His mother's boyfriend was one of the main drug dealers in the community. His cousin C.J. lived on the second floor above the chapel. Robbie and C.J.'s family were involved in the "business" in this notorious building.

Robbie's grandmother actively practiced Santeria. Her altar and idols were located right above our chapel. Often-times she would bang the floor and make noises to disturb us when we began activities or Bible study.

The building was decrepit. There was limited heat in the winter. Broken windows were rarely replaced and plumbing rarely repaired. Rats infested the area and came indoors during the colder months. Visiting one of the apartments, I noticed very odd-looking molding where the walls met the ceiling. It was about an inch wide and wrapped completely around the main room of the apartment. Getting closer to it, I realized it was roaches, caked and crawling together in masses. The stench from all these things was nearly unbearable.

Robbie would come to his grandmother's apartment after school. We met him and C.J. and invited them to come to our children's outreach. C.J. had a bubbly personality. Robbie rarely spoke and never looked anyone in the eyes. Sometimes he came with evidence of abuse. A bruise on his face or head was explained by falling down the stairs or a snowball fight.

We loved these children. We prayed for them and built relationships with their families, knowing that the greatest way for God to impact the children's lives was for Him to impact the entire family. We earned their trust as the genuine love of God began to pour into their lives. That love deeply touched their hearts.

They also observed our behaviors. Like hawks, the people in the community observed our movements, our interactions, and everything about us. They talked among themselves about us, and they analyzed our conversations. They took their time observing this new couple and the "white guy" setting up shop in their community. It helped that Lidia is from Chile and that I am fluent in Spanish. Even so, it took three years or more for some of the people to become open to us.

Lidia and I met a mother in the projects whom we had never seen. As we introduced ourselves, she said, "Oh, I know who you are. We've been watching you for three years. We know what you do. We know where you go. We know the apartments you eat in and the people that prepare your food. That's why we trust you." There were a few families who would invite us for meals in their home. One of the women who prepared our food had AIDS. Praying over meals was real prayer for us. The people in the community saw us visiting these homes and eating with these families. It gave them confidence in us and openness to hear the message of hope in Jesus Christ that we were bringing to them.

Occasional signs of abuse in Robbie continued, placing us in an awkward situation. According to the law, we had to report any signs of abuse or we would be held liable if anything happened to a child. We were greatly concerned for the boy but also concerned about violating the relationship of trust we were building not only with his family but with everyone in the community. We knew the results would be devastating if it was found out that we had reported a mother and her boyfriend, especially someone involved in the "trade." All trust would be destroyed not just with them, but with everyone.

We prayed. Then we prayed more. After several days, we came to the conclusion that we could do no other but call in a report and pray it would remain anonymous.

Before we made the phone call, the most amazing thing happened. Robbie's mother, Darla, called us. She invited us to her apartment. We quickly and gladly accepted.

Angel played in their living room with Robbie and his younger brother. Darla invited us into the little kitchen and offered us some coffee. My conversations with her had always been brief, but on many occasions, Lidia had encouraged her with God's love for her and her children. As we sat down together at her little table, Darla began to speak:

"There are only three people in this entire world that I trust: my mother and the two of you." Darla began to cry as she shared about her life situation and sought our counsel. Our counsel began with God's unconditional love for her.

We were amazed at God. We were also thankful for Him preventing us from making that report. Instead, He who is in control of all things was in control of this thing, and He began to make something beautiful from it. Signs of abuse ended. Robbie began to look into our eyes and have conversations with us. He began to improve in school and in his behavior, so much so that his grandmother came downstairs and confronted us one day to express her gratitude to us for our work, She said, "I don't know what you do, but it's working because Robbie is better than he was."

The banging on the ceiling from the apartment upstairs stopped after that.

In His home synagogue, Jesus opened the scriptures to the writings of the prophet Isaiah and read:

"The Spirit of the Sovereign LORD is upon Me, for the LORD has anointed Me to bring good news to the poor. He has sent Me to comfort the brokenhearted and to proclaim that captives will be released and prisoners will be freed. He has sent Me to tell those who mourn that the time of the LORD's favor has come, and with it the day of God's anger against His enemies. To all who mourn in Israel, He will give a crown of beauty for ashes, a joyous blessing instead of mourning, festive praise instead of despair" (Isaiah 61:1-3).

This passage and the ensuing verses have become central to our work. Here is the way it has impacted us:

The Spirit of the Sovereign LORD is upon Jesus in us, and the LORD has anointed us to bring the Good News to the poor. He has sent us with His message and love to comfort the brokenhearted (and there are so many around us) *and to proclaim that those in spiritual bondage and in prisons of emotions and addictions and fear can be set free. He has sent us to tell those who mourn over the violence and suffering around them and the ways it has affected them that the time of the LORD's favor and blessing has come through the cross and empty tomb, and with it, the day of God's anger against the enemy of their souls. To all who mourn in this community, Jesus will give a crown of beauty for ashes, a joyous blessing instead of sorrow, and hope instead of despair.*

This is why God sent us to the South Bronx.

The passage continues with more purpose of our ministry:

"In their righteousness, they will be like great oaks that the LORD has planted for His own glory. They will rebuild the ancient ruins, repairing cities destroyed long ago. They will revive them, though they

have been deserted for many generations" (Isaiah 61:3-4, emphasis mine).

This is our mission - to see the poor and suffering, those without hope, raised up like *strong and graceful oaks for the Lord's glory,* and to empower them to be those who *repair cities long ago destroyed.*

"I knew you before you were formed in your mother's womb. Before you were born, I set you apart and appointed you..." (Jeremiah 1:5). Before we were born, He set us apart and ordained a purpose for our lives! A divinely designed destiny is prepared for every individual, no matter their background, family, community, suffering, lack of opportunity or anything else. In love and divine intervention, God will mold them to be *strong and graceful oaks for His own glory.*

But love must involve action to change lives. God formed our mission to focus on five things to break generational strongholds and propel people toward their destinies: 1) faith, 2) values and right choices, 3) family responsibility, 4) work ethic and 5) education. Our programming, mentoring, discipleship and counseling would continually reinforce these things.

While it may appear appealing to have several hundred people lining up outside your doors for a free lunch, God called us to minister differently. He challenged us: how do we really make a difference in this community? How do we effectively touch individuals and families? We must provide people with what they really need. So, we focused on individuals, not piling everyone into a pre-made plan, but through relationships, identifying the real needs in their lives and the best pathway to realize their destinies. Through that, and in relationship with Jesus Christ, they would own the hope and joy that had always been out of reach.

We believe this is the core of how we change the inner city or any place in the world in need of hope and redemption - *one person and one family at a time.* It is a different approach from what many assume is ordinary "inner city ministry," but as a friend said in observation of our outreach, "Until we change the hearts and minds of people, we can throw everything at them but it won't help." We can give them clothes and give them food, but if they can't read and write, if they have no job skills, if their lives are in disarray, if they can't graduate from high school . . . , they will always be waiting in that line.

We began an after-school tutoring program with eight teenagers. The numbers quickly grew as these teens enjoyed a safe environment of unconditional love and shared about it with their peers. They ran to *The Harvest Center* after school, often bringing friends with them. This became their home, and we became their family.

We spread the news and donations of textbooks, reading books and school supplies poured in. We even received a microscope and slides from a science laboratory in Charlotte. Our intentions were to provide instruction in English, Math, Science and History. I spent a lot of time planning and preparing the classes with my wife and an intern. We were excited to start! I began the first day with a simple exercise in English. I learned at that moment that they could not write a paragraph with a topic sentence. This was not because of a lack of ability, but because of a lack of opportunity and academic support. We set aside all other subjects and focused only on English.

For months, we read and wrote. After just a couple months, we began to see changes. Teachers were complimenting the students on their schoolwork. Grades improved. They received academic awards. This affected everything: self-worth, confidence, hope for the future, vision for their lives, family relationships, and faith in a God whose Word must be true: *"I can do everything through Christ, who gives me strength"* (Philippians 4:13).

Many of our students became the first in their families to receive a high school diploma. In a community where 85 percent of students drop out of high school, for the first 12 years of our tutoring programs, over 97 percent of our students graduated high school on time and went to college. This was not because we were the greatest tutors. It was because of what they found at *The Harvest*

Center: a place where they felt safe, where they were accepted, where they were challenged, where people cared, loved enough to hold them accountable with their schoolwork, and demonstrated pride over their progress reports and report cards. This made an eternal difference in their lives.

We then began an after-school program for the children called *Kidz Klub* which combined fun, nutrition, academics and spiritual enrichment for children 7-12 years old. This presented new challenges. In the three junior high schools closest to us, less than 10 percent of eighth graders read at grade level. In the closest junior high school just a few blocks down Brook Avenue, 1.5 percent of eighth graders read at grade level. We poured into the children the best we could and began to see the same kinds of changes we saw with the teens.

A five-year-old girl came to Kidz Klub one day. She was too young for our programs. When we heard her story, we were compelled to break the rules and make Vanessa a part of Kidz Klub. We did not anticipate that she would quickly become a part of our family. Being of the same age as my daughter, the two of them became like sisters.

Vanessa was a child without a future. She was "destined" to fail. Her junior high school counselor once told her to drop out of school because, "you're just going to be a drug dealer like your brother." Despite the obstacles she faced, with the love and support she found at Harvest and the tenacity to never give up, Vanessa rose above the expectations of people like that counselor. She finished high school, and college, and post-graduate work, and she is leading a thriving life. She developed a God-given gift on computers. She did many videos for Urban Harvest, served in ministry to the children and helped lead outreaches for years. Oh, how we thank God for His work in her life!

Vanessa's mother, Joanna, had a tough childhood. At nine-years-old, Joanna's aunt took her to Alcoholics Anonymous because she already had a drinking problem. By twelve years old, she was addicted to heroin, driven to drugs and alcohol by the abuse in her home. We would sometimes find Vanessa wandering the streets near midnight, looking for her mother. Joanna has four children, with Vanessa being the youngest. She told me once that, because of heroin, she did not remember the birth of two of her four children.

We talked with Joanna every chance we had. We attempted numerous times to visit her in her home. She was resistant to help, completely opposed to the opportunity to change because of the bondage of addiction. After thirteen years of knowing her and praying for her, she walked into the Friday night ladies group my wife had started, threw the door open and said, "I'm ready." Lidia and a couple of her leaders jumped up, not knowing if she was ready to fight someone. Lidia walked up to her and asked, "You're ready for what, Joanna?"

Joanna replied, "I'm ready for God to change my life."

Her addiction lasted 42 years, but by the touch of God's grace on a desperate life, that came to an end. Not only that, but members of her family began to come to faith in Christ and attend church with her. In one of the most moving moments of our ministry, Joanna's daughter Sandy came to the ladies' fellowship to see what this was that had impacted her mother in such a profound way. Sandy was bitter toward her mother, understandably so with the pain her mother had caused the family. All the sudden, Sandy jumped up from her seat and launched toward her mother. Before anyone could react, Sandy fell at her mother's feet, wrapped her arms around her mother's legs and said, "I love you, Mommy." For the first time in Sandy's life, Joanna reached down, embraced her daughter and said, "I love you, too."

He will bring beauty from ashes, joy instead of mourning, and hope in place of despair.

As a result of our tutoring programs and the effect on the lives of these youth, God opened doors in area schools. My academic degrees and experience in education were respected in our community. I was not viewed as a pastor but a former university professor with a doctorate who was helping youth in the community. Yet the community knew we were a faith- based organization. Despite that, they opened the doors of their schools. Twice in three years we held concerts with Christian artists at the South Bronx Community Action Theater, which was part of our school district. On each occasion, the office sent invitations to all area schools and parent-teacher associations, encouraging them to come and hear the message of hope and faith that we would bring at their theater. Both concerts were a huge success. At the end of the concerts, the area in front of the stage filled with people desiring prayer and life change.

I was invited to speak for Career Day at South Bronx High School, which was just a few blocks from *The Harvest Center.* I did so for six years, looking students in the eyes and challenging them about their life choices and their destinies. God gave favor the first year and opened the door for us to begin a Bible Club for the students. Then the door opened through another group of our students to begin a Bible Club in a high school in Manhattan. In God's design, the high school in Manhattan hosted the *Symposium on Equality and Justice* on Martin Luther King Jr. Day, and I was invited to speak. In every opportunity, I shared my beliefs about the hope and divine destiny that was within their grasp.

The second year at the *Symposium*, I shared Martin Luther King Jr.'s words from his compelling *Letter from Birmingham Jail* written to fellow clergymen defending his Biblical mission and purpose for peaceful protest. As I was reading King's words, a man in the lecture hall stood up and interrupted me saying, "You can't do this! You can't say these things! This is a public school." I thought he was a teacher but later learned he was a lawyer with the New York ACLU. My biggest surprise, however, was not in this man's interruption but in the response that it sparked from the students.

Students began to shout the man down, yelling at him from all over the lecture hall.

After a few moments, a female student toward the back of the lecture hall stood up. Speaking to the lawyer, she said, "Sir, nobody makes us believe anything. We are the ones who decide what we want to believe." Then pointing to me, she said, "We want to hear what he has to say!"

We want to hear what he has to say.

The words sent a chill through the core of my being. Here, in a public high school in Manhattan, with an ACLU lawyer trying to halt my lecture, a student spoke for all the students there, sharing their desire to hear a message that was lighting a fire in their hearts. Through this young lady, God gave me the freedom to finish my lecture, and to expand on it with my belief in their destinies, ordained by God and discovered through a relationship with Him.

By God's divine providence, and perhaps by the cunning of the vice-principal in charge of the symposium, I was seated by that lawyer for lunch later that day. We had a very pleasant conversation, with him humbly asking questions not as a lawyer but as a creation of God wondering about His Maker.

I wondered what seeds were sown that day. In one of my meetings with Pastor Dave Wilkerson in the first year of our work, he said to me, "Tom, don't ever think that you will establish a church like Times Square in the South Bronx. That is not why God brought you there. You will establish a spiritual hospital. Many people will come through your doors, sometimes only once, but it will be the step that begins the change in their lives."

Marie was a kind and beautiful teenager who heard me speak at Career Day at South Bronx High School. She became a part of our youth programs at Harvest and was endeared to our family. Yet, we did not know the painful and dark secret that was hiding in her heart.

Marie came to *The Harvest Center* one day during our after-school program. We thought she was coming for the tutoring/ mentoring program, but that was not the case. She was agitated and in quite a bit of a hurry as she asked if she could speak to Lidia and me privately.

Marie informed us that she was running away from home that day. The abuse in her home was so bad for so long she couldn't take it anymore. We pled with her to stay and allow us to help her, but she could not go back home one more day. She came by to thank us for what we had done for her and to give us a loving goodbye. I ran to my office, grabbed a Bible, wrote a little something to her on the dedication page and gave it to her. We prayed for her, hugged her, and said goodbye. Our hearts were broken for days over this.

We didn't hear from Marie for many years, twelve to be exact. Then one day we received a phone call. Marie was back in the Bronx and wanted to see us. We met her and her husband and heard her story. Here is their story in Marie's own words.

My name is Marie. In 1995, I moved to the Bronx. My family life was very abusive, and my life was very hopeless. I attended Career Day at South Bronx High School. Dr. Tom Grassano was a guest speaker. I was moved and decided to start going to his church. I never felt more at home and more loved than like I did at Harvest. I had finally found a place where I felt a sense of belonging.

At home, things got worse. As I found out about my mother's drug use, the physical abuse worsened, and my grades dropped quickly. I couldn't take it any longer, so I decided to drop out of high school and run away.

I came back to the Bronx in April of 2001 with a child and a recent divorce to try to have a new beginning. I stayed with my mother but quickly I realized that family life was still the same. I started going to Harvest once more. Once again, I felt at peace there, but returning to my mother's house each night proved to be unbearable for me, so once more I decided to leave. The Grassano's begged me not to leave, but I felt a sense of urgency to get out of my situation at home. I was too embarrassed to tell anyone what was going on. Instead, I chose to keep it to myself and put on a strong face. Before I left, Pastor Tom gave me a Bible in which he wrote "To Marie, From Pastor Tom and Lidia...God bless you always! We love you!" I said my goodbyes and went on my way.

Years passed. Temptation disguised itself in very attractive packages. I married a second time, endured an abusive relationship, birthed my second child, was diagnosed with TB and went through a second divorce. I was in such a dark place with pain like no other. I was angry at the world and far removed from God.

I entered into a relationship with a young man named Keith, and we moved to New Orleans. A few months later, I gave birth to our son. I soon started to experiment in drugs and alcohol. It all caught up with us, and shortly after, our children were taken from us. We couldn't make ends meet, so we found ourselves being evicted from our apartment and sleeping on the floor of random friends' homes for months. We tried getting back on our feet, but it seemed that every effort was fruitless. Hurricane Katrina wiped us out and forced us to move to Orange County, Texas. As we were trying to rebuild our lives, Hurricane Rita wiped out everything in the area and finding a job became impossible.

We moved back to New Orleans trying to straighten up our act, but our efforts were fruitless. We went through a downward spiral of alcohol and drugs and felt like we were lost without a cause. Nothing was going right. We were living selfishly with anger and hurt and justifying everything we did because of what had happened and how we felt. Only when we realized that we had had enough, God intervened!

I started praying and asked God to forgive my disobedience and to please come back into my life. As I was going through some boxes in our friend's garage, I came to a box that I had not seen for a very long time. I opened it and I saw a familiar brown Bible. In the inscription it read, "To Marie, From Pastor Tom and Lidia...God bless you always! We love you!" I was blown away by God's grace, compassion, love, and TIMING! Only God knew how much I needed those words, and only He knew what He was doing when Pastor chose to give me that Bible and wrote those specific words years before!

I asked God to please touch my boyfriend's heart and let him walk closer to Jesus. I wanted Keith to KNOW God and to form a deep and meaningful relationship with the Lord. One day, many months later, Keith fell into a deep depression that no one could really understand. I stayed beside him, praying and asking God to soften Keith's heart, and to reveal Himself to us….to show us the truth of His love and grace.

Keith spent a week or so in bed without hardly eating or sleeping. One morning, he came to me and started telling me how he felt about our present life and that living for ourselves wasn't sufficient anymore. He said that we neededto put God FIRST in our lives, and if we were to live right in His eyes, we needed to do so right then and there. I started crying and praised God because He had answered my prayers!

Keith and I chose to leave our old lives behind and make a complete about face and serve the Lord on the spot! A week or two later, we sold everything we had. We put what little we did keep (including that brown Bible) in two backpacks and two duffel bags and left everything to come to the South Bronx. Our intentions were to visit my family and seek out Pastor Tom and his guidance before continuing on our way to find God's plan for us. I felt so desperate for the same kind of love and acceptance like before … even better! The hunger inside of me for the Word of God was, and still is, so great that I nearly jumped out of my skin.

We met Pastor Tom and Sister Lidia at The Harvest Center. Upon speaking with him and receiving too many signs to count, we realized THIS was exactly where God had intended for us to be. Our lives have been forever changed and all the glory is for God because He has brought me back to the place where I first started to learn of His Word. I'm so grateful for what He is doing in our lives. It doesn't matter what I've done or where I've come from, God has the power to do great things. God truly has changed our lives. I found an indescribable abundance of peace and happiness in my life that I can only attribute to submitting to God and accepting Jesus Christ as my Lord and Savior! I pray that His light shines in me brightly so that others can see it miles away and get to know God's truth, so that they too can turn their lives around, so that they can be a witness for Him.

We had a beautiful reunion the day that Keith and Marie came back to the Bronx.

God gave us the blessings of growing in relationship with them and mentoring them for a few years. Feeling a need to help Keith's family in New Orleans, they moved back to his home. Keith began Bible school and became a youth pastor in a local church. A job transfer moved them to another city. They are on their faith journey, pursuing their destinies in Christ. We still rejoice over the miracle Bible that lasted through twelve years of instability and crises to remind Marie of God's loving purpose for her and for Keith.

Just as the Word says that God will restore what the locust has eaten, God replaced lost children with three beautiful children, a son and two daughters. Their precious son is named after me.

God truly is so good.

Chapter Seven

Corruption and Redemption

"You intended to harm me, but God intended it all for good ... for the salvation of many."

Joseph in Genesis 50:20

It took significant time to make a dent in the stone-cold faces of the drug dealers. At first, they observed me closely to see if I was a "Fed." There had been other occasions when undercover cops posed as priests and even once as a nun, so a white man saying he was there to serve was not terribly convincing.

Winning their confidence would be no small task. It helped that we had worked in the community for three years before moving there. They knew our faces and had observed our outreach. They respected our work with the children. Nevertheless, it was not beyond their imagination that the whole thing could be a setup. Trust was not easy to earn here.

Conversations with the drug dealers began about a year into our work. I would always acknowledge them, smile and say hello, but they gave no response, usually not even looking at me. The first breakthrough happened when I said hello to one and he nodded his head with a simple lift of the chin. I was amazed. This had never happened before. To the outside observer it would be nothing, but knowing their culture and lack of trust, this was a huge breakthrough.

After several months, the nod of the chin grew to deeper conversations with me saying "Hello!" and their response being a nod and "'Sup?"

Slowly but surely things grew as they would initiate the conversation. "'Sup?" I would respond, "What's up?" Their response would always be, "Chillin."

One of the main dealers nicknamed "Blue Eyes" had a girlfriend who was Robbie's mother. Robbie's two aunts lived in the apartment upstairs with his grandmother. Both aunts had boyfriends who were drug dealers. God had put us in *the* notorious building in the community. (The post office refused to deliver mail in this building!) Stuff was going on every day. We realized God had divinely placed us there. God wanted us to set up shop on that block for those souls.

We learned Robbie had a birthday in July, shortly after our daughter's birthday. We decided to have a birthday party for both of them. We didn't realize how powerfully this would speak to Robbie's family and Blue Eyes.

As we were cleaning up after the party, I noticed there were some cold sodas left over. Suddenly, I heard the Lord speak to my heart and say: "The drug dealers across the street are hot and thirsty. Go serve them some cold soda."

I hesitated for a moment, praying and wanting to make sure this was the Lord's voice. We already had great opposition from organized religion in the community. Cops had harassed me on the street, for which I cannot blame them. In their minds, it was suspicious that some white guy was hanging out in their community and talking with drug dealers on street corners. I grabbed a cold soda, some cups and paper towels, and headed across the street, noting that God said, "serve them" not "give them soda."

"You guys look hot out here. Here's some cold soda for you." I served the soda in a cup with a paper towel, saying to each one, "God bless you."

They looked at me with bewilderment. You could see in their eyes, "Who is this guy? What's he doing this for?" I finished serving the last one and told them I would leave the soda bottle for them. I said, "God bless you guys!" as I walked away.

After that infamous day in Darla's apartment when she said, "There are only three people in the entire world that I trust: my mother and both of you," relationships with the family grew. More and more, they allowed us into their apartments and allowed us to speak the truth to them about their lifestyles and about the love of Christ that could change everything. They embraced us as one of their family, which opened the door to stronger relationships with the drug dealers.

The children began to change. They changed in their behavior, in their respect, in their schoolwork, and in their communication. God was beginning to bring fruit from our labors.

Other people noticed our involvement with these families. While entering the building to visit their apartment one day, I was confronted by three leaders of a church in the community. "We've concluded that you are not a minister, and we want to know what you do."

"Why do you say that?" I asked.

They responded, "We've been watching you. There's no way you could be a minister and go to these apartments and hang out with the people you hang out with. You're not a minister."

I became choked up. I responded, "Thank you. Thank you for saying that. That means a lot to me," and I walked up the stairs to an apartment. I waited at the landing of the second floor to wipe a few tears before knocking at the door. Those men did not realize it, but they had given me the highest compliment. They had accused me of being like Jesus.

Setting up for Kidz Klub one Saturday, I was amazed when Blue Eyes walked in. He came straight to me and said, "Me and Darla are going to Brooklyn today. I may have to get Robbie before you finish. I just want you to know because I don't want todisrespect you in any way. If I come in to get him, that's why."

That was a breakthrough! Our conversation just elevated from "'Sup" and "Chillin." I thanked him. He came back later, respectfully and discreetly removing Robbie for their day trip.

Conversations began to grow after that. It was not anything deep. We would talk about the weather, about the Yankees, and about the kids. I would inform them of events taking place, like block parties and dinners. I would always invite them to these things and to our worship and Bible studies, encouraging them to come. Once, two of them, Craze and Manny, came into the chapel toward the end of a Bible study on a Wednesday night. They stayed almost an hour, touched by the presence of the Lord in that place. Craze said, "I've never felt anything like this before," and then he sat silently for nearly half an hour soaking in the presence of the Lord.

The others never came, but they seemed to appreciate the invitations. Through our conversations and my prayers for them, my love began to grow for them, as did my realization of the destiny they could have if they changed their ways.

I learned that Blue Eyes had overdosed. He was in the psych ward of a Bronx hospital, so I went to visit him. I gave his real name and my identification. "What is your relation?" they asked.

"I'm his pastor."

I stood in the hallway until Blue Eyes appeared. We locked eyes as he walked straight toward me with no expression on his face. I didn't know what response my visit would bring. As he came to me, I put my hand out to shake his hand. Instead, he wrapped both arms around me and cried on my shoulder.

We spoke for hours. I went back each day until he was released from the hospital.

We talked about his family and his background, and I talked about mine. I learned about his interests, likes and dislikes, and he learned about mine. We talked about his choices, the consequences they had brought into his life, and the hope Christ could bring in their place. I shared our reason for being in the Bronx, making sure he understood our purpose and our calling from God.

I wanted to bring hope into his life. The first steps were to get to know each other on a deeper level. Conversations were open and honest, sometimes painfully honest. I bathed every word with unconditional love yet never backed down one inch from my faith and convictions. Trust was the result, and that opened new doors of influence.

Blue Eyes wanted to continue our conversations after he was released from the hospital, but he didn't want his crew to know he was meeting with "the pastor" to talk. We agreed to meet in the mornings at 9:00 am, before the dealers were awake. (Since they "work" until many hours after midnight each night, they live like third shift workers, sleeping in the mornings.)

I was a little skeptical on the way to our first meeting, doubtful that he would even come and if he did, thinking he would be late and with an excuse why he could not stay. To my surprise, he was waiting at the door of the chapel when I arrived a few minutes before 9:00. We did as we did in the hospital, talking about baseball, relationships, his health, his choices and his soul. We opened the Bible, and I began to share more deeply about God's loving purpose for Him. We ended every meeting in prayer.

Our meetings became regular, often several times a week. He finally came to a Sunday service with his girlfriend and baby, and they were made part of the spiritual family. Our personal meetings continued but one thing changed: He asked me to bring my guitar. He loved the song *"Create in Me a Clean Heart"* and asked me to sing it to him frequently. It was a song that expressed his feelings to God.

Blue Eyes really tried to get his life together but there were some huge obstacles. A prayer request quickly became a frustration. *"How can I ever get a job with this criminal record?"* he would ask. Weeks went by with no change.

My relationship with Blue Eyes gave me a new relationship with the guys on the street. We talked and the trust level grew. Conversations became deeper and more frequent. Blue Eyes just couldn't find a job. His friends began to give him some cash to help his family. Eventually, he was drawn back into his former lifestyle, but our relationship had become strong and I continued to show him unconditional love.

These things set the stage for a major event that would begin with a letter. The letter was from our precinct, inviting me to a clergy meeting with the precinct captain, community affairs officer and a representative from the Bronx District Attorney. When I received the invitation, I immediately discarded it. It didn't fit into the things that were a priority to us. After all, I was trying to win the hearts of drug dealers and drug addicts and people on the streets. A close affiliation with the police would not be of benefit to me, either ministry-wise or even for personal safety.

Our precinct had a reputation, and it was not a good one. I had been harassed on the street, but I could understand. I was the first white man in the community in years that was not a cop, a landlord or a homeless drug addict. Youth were harassed by cops on the street. Sometimes good kids were busted for possession when they had nothing in their pockets until the cops stuck it in there. Robberies and smaller crimes would bring no investigation. For example, when a youth center near us was broken into and had their computers stolen, cops came four days later to check it out. Rumors were that dirty cops would bust drug dealers and then take their drugs and money and give the drugs to other dealers to sell with them receiving a cut. Ten cops were eventually arrested for this very thing.

For all these reasons, I had no intention of going to that meeting, but God would not leave me alone. I dug the invitation out of the garbage.

I fussed with God for two weeks. "I'm not going, God. I'm not going!" I think He just chuckled as He said, "Yes, you are." I finally told God I would go, but I assured Him, "I will not say anything; I will just sit there."

At least, that was my plan.

I arrived at the meeting. The room had clergy sitting in a semicircle around a table with two chairs. The precinct captain, community affairs officer and Bronx D.A. sat at the table and began their presentation, first talking about how important we as clergy are in the community, and then sharing how they need our help to clean drugs off the streets. "People are afraid of retribution. That's why they don't turn in drug dealers. We need you to assist us by turning in drug dealers and keeping us informed on the activity around your churches."

They continued with their presentation. Then they gave the clergy a time to respond. Each clergyman there affirmed that he would help as the police had requested.

I was literally squirming in my chair. Words welled up in me, but I fought against it. I had already told God I would say nothing. My heart began beating harder the more I resisted. I begged God to leave me alone, but I knew He had a purpose in me being there that day, whether I approved or not.

I finally spoke.

"First of all, we believe that the Bible teaches us that we are to pray for all people in authority over us. As police and the District Attorney, you have authority in this community. We pray for you and we teach our people to pray for you.

"Secondly, we are not going to turn in drug dealers. Our job is not to turn them in to you. Our job is to see their lives changed so you won't have to worry about them anymore."

The countenances of the captain and rep from the D.A. completely changed. You could see their frustration with my comments. They whispered to one another. Then the D.A. rep began writing something down. I sensed that he was making notes by my name.

I was not done speaking.

"You say the people of this community are afraid of retribution and for that reason they don't turn in drug dealers, but you have said nothing about the lack of integrity and corruption in this precinct. I have only been here for a few years, but I can tell you that from the smallest child to the oldest grandmother, nobody trusts you."

I then mentioned the names of a couple cops I knew who were people of integrity, cops who loved the community and the people and wanted to repair the relationship between the community and the precinct. "You have to get these cops and cops like them on the streets to rebuild relationships of trust and integrity with this community."

I vividly remember the rest of my words: "Your position is ordained of God just like my position is ordained of God. If I do not carry out the authority God has given me according to the character and integrity taught in His Word, He will judge me. If you do not carry out the authority God has given you according to the character and integrity in His Word, there is no review board and no disciplinary committee that will do to you what God will do to you when He judges you."

They were upset, but I was at peace. I had stated what needed to be stated, and I did so calmly and with a respectful tone of voice.

Two weeks later, the cops busted all the drug dealers in our area and told them I was the one that ratted them out. Of course, I did not. It appeared that they did this to rid themselves of me by whatever means necessary.

I was alone in the chapel after a Bible class on a Wednesday night, packing up my things and preparing to turn the lights off and lock up. Then Blue Eyes walked in and came straight up to me.

"You need to stay away for a while. The cops busted everybody and told us you ratted us out. You need to get away. You know what it's like here. The guys have guns with them all the time. You need to go away for a few weeks until things calm down."

I was startled by the news but blessed and amazed that he cared that much to tell me.

"Thank you for informing me, but I can't do that."

"You have to. You are in danger." Blue Eyes nodded, shook my hand and walked out of the building.

I was amazed that Blue Eyes had taken the risk to inform me of what was circulating on the streets. This showed his respect and concern for me. He didn't want me harmed and he took a chance to come and tell me before something happened.

I was not afraid. This was not some brazen boldness or stupidity. I simply had the peace of God and a calm assurance that I would be fine. I went home that night, prayed, and went to sleep.

The next morning, I arrived at *The Harvest Center* about 9:30 am., long before the dealers are on the streets. As I parked my car and got out, one of the dealers came out of the building, two more came around the corner on the left, and four others started walking toward me from down the block. Blue Eyes was one of them.

As two of them came close, I grabbed one by the arm and said, "Buy me an ice cream. I need to talk to you guys."

He looked at me with the most puzzled look on his face and said, "Huh?"

"That's right. Buy me an ice cream. I need to talk to you guys."

"At this time of the morning?"

We walked to the corner and he bought me an ice cream. Seven of the guys were there. No one spoke. It was my time to speak.

Matthew 10:19 in The Message Bible says, *"And don't worry about what you'll say or how you'll say it. The right words will be there; the Spirit of your Father will supply the words."* God proved His Word to me that day.

"I've heard what's been said. I didn't do it. But I am not here today to try to convince you about something I did or didn't do. I want to make sure you know why I am here in this community."

From that point, I began to explain my calling there, where I came from, and what we understood as God's purposes for us. For a long 20 minutes, they stood silently, listening closely to my words.

Then I concluded. "You say the white man oppresses this community. I've been here for three years and I have never seen a white man standing on a street corner selling drugs to your mothers and fathers and your brothers and sisters. You are.

"I hate what you do. I despise what you do. God hates what you do. But I love you and believe in who you could become if you would put your faith in Jesus Christ and let God change you."

The next words I heard amazed me! They were not the words I had anticipated at all, for I truly didn't know what would happen next.

One of them nicknamed "Gordo" spoke up and said, "Pastor Tom . . . " They had never called me "Pastor!" They rarely even called me "Tom." This was a breakthrough greater than I could have ever hoped for!

"Pastor Tom, we know you didn't do this. We'll take care of it. Don't you worry."

Then he said: "You're different from all of the other pastors here. You treat us with respect. You invite us to your services. You invite us to your dinners and block parties. Hell, you even served us cold soda when we were hustlin' on the street.

"We see you have people visiting you helping you out sometimes. You just let us know what cars belong to them, and we will take care of them. And we won't sell drugs in front of your building anymore.

If anyone bothers you, you let us know." He paused a moment, and then continued, "Thank you for what you're doin' here."

Then each one shook my hand, South Bronx-style, from the heart.

He called me pastor. He recognized how I had been treating them, including serving them soda after the birthday party over a year before. He confessed with his mouth that they sell drugs but said they would not do it in front of our building. He verbalized his respect. *What a miracle!*

They kept their word. They quit selling drugs in front of our building.

I could leave my car unlocked and not worry about it. One day, a man was yelling obscenities in front of our storefront to someone in an apartment above while Kidz Klub was in session. Some of the guys took the man around the corner and taught him a lesson for disrespecting our place.

A new day had dawned for us in the Bronx.

Six years later, I learned more of what really happened that day. One of the dealers had disappeared for a couple years. I learned to not ask questions but wondered what had happened to him as he had occupied many of our prayers. He walked into my office, smiled, took off his hat and said, "I love what you did to our building!"

He sat in my office and began to share about how God had changed his life. He left for his grandmother's home in Florida to get out of the community. With tears in his eyes, he said to me, "If it wasn't for my grandmother's prayers and you, Lidia and Angel's prayers, I don't know where I would be right now. I'd probably be dead or locked up."

I didn't want Lidia to hear this from me, so I asked him if I could call her and put him on the phone with her. He agreed. I called Lidia and handed him the phone. Before he took the phone into his hands, he stood up, removed his hat, and straightened his jacket. Then with tears, he told Lidia about the changes in his life and thanked her and Angel for their prayers.

I informed him that I would be visiting Florida shortly after that to speak at a youth conference. He begged me to come to his home so that he could prepare a meal for me. When I arrived at the entrance of the mobile home park, he was waiting for me. We enjoyed a wonderful meal together. We sat down afterwards to talk for quite a while. During our conversation, I said, "Do you remember that time the cops arrested all of you and said I had ratted you out?"

His response surprised me.

"Oh, it wasn't us that wanted to kill you. That was________" and he named a South Bronx rapper who is the main drug supplier for our community.

The real story of what happened was that word traveled up the ladder to the supplier. When he heard it, he put a "hit" on me, ordering my death.

"What happened?" I asked.

"After we met with you that day, we sent Jingo (one of the dealers) to (the rapper) and he told him, 'If you try to do anything to Pastor Tom, you have to go through us first.'"

That's what they meant when they said, "Don't worry. We'll take care of this." God used these guys that we had come to love to save my life.

Today, these guys are my friends, like family. Some are like adopted sons. Sadly, Gordo, the spokesman in our meeting on the street, is dead, a casualty of his lifestyle and another among many who was robbed of his future. Sonny is working a great job and spoiling his grandson. He is a true friend and a man with a tender heart who seeks to honor God. Joseph, Blue Eye's brother, became a teacher. God reunited us before Joseph's tragic death. Adrian, or "Craze," is a wonderful father and husband, raising all his nine children to make right choices. Under his strong exterior is a heart that genuinely loves his family and friends. He is a hard-working man with faith in God.

A few years ago, a 13-year-old girl approached me after Kidz Klub and asked for the lyrics to the song, *"Create in Me a Clean Heart."* I was puzzled as I didn't ever remember singing that song in Kidz Klub. I had her come to my office and I quickly typed the lyrics on the computer and printed it for her.

While I did, she said, "This is for a friend of my mother. You know him. His name is Victor." I knew many people by that name. I asked her to clarify.

She said, "You called him Blue Eyes."

My mouth dropped open and I stopped typing. I turned to her in amazement.

Blue Eyes was serving a long sentence in jail and had been diagnosed with brain cancer. He remembered hearing me sing *"Create in Me a Clean Heart."* It touched him deeply. He spoke to a friend and asked her daughter to get the lyrics from me. He wanted to put the words of the song in his jail cell.

Remember Robbie's grandmother, the Santeria witch who would beat the floors when we began Bible studies? We received word from her daughters that she had died. Lidia and I acquired details of the funeral arrangements and went to visit the family. On the way, we commented to ourselves about how this woman's soul must be in hell for the way she lived and the witchcraft in which she was involved.

When we arrived at the funeral home, the daughters and family approached us with warm hugs. It was so good to see them, despite the circumstances. Then one of the daughters said, "You don't know what happened to my mother, do you?" They had moved from the community, and we had not had contact with them.

"She came to God. She burned all her idols. She read the Bible and prayed every day and constantly told us that we need to get our lives right with God."

God is constantly moving, constantly working, constantly doing things that we do not see to accomplish His purposes and bring glory to His name. When we think He is not moving and working, He still is, preparing hearts and souls for their next steps in Him.

In the early years of our work in the South Bronx, many people questioned our wisdom of taking our daughter with us. Angel accompanied us in all situations. She played in the playgrounds with the kids. She attended the children's programs we started. She went with us when we visited people's apartments. Both of my children grew up with this ministry being part of their everyday lives.

Over 15 years into our work in the Bronx, we learned what made the dealers believe that I was who I said I was. It wasn't a particular outreach event or something that I said or did. It was that Angel was with me. They realized I had to be who I said I was because no one else would bring his little daughter into that community like I did.

When my daughter Angel was only four years old, she began to pray for Spike. Sometimes she would walk to the door of the chapel, catch his eye and wave hello to him while he was doing business on the street. We didn't know this until many years later when we learned how much that had touched him.

In December 2011, he called my office. "Tom, what time are the services at your church?" I informed him of the service times and said, "We have prayer tonight at 6:30 pm." He replied, "I'll change my shirt and be right there" and he hung up. I held the phone in my hand looking at it and wondering if I heard him right. After 17 years of praying for him, loving him and speaking the truth, could this be true?

When 6:30 arrived, he came into the chapel and sat down. After a time of prayer, I invited him down to my office and he began to share:

"I reached the place where I just couldn't do this anymore. I prayed Sunday and just asked God for help, and when I did, I felt like something warm just poured all over me. I felt peace." Christ became the Lord of this tender-hearted man. I had the privilege of baptizing him. A wonderful father and hard worker, he strives to be faithful to God. He is raising his daughter as a loving, faithful father. My children call him "Uncle Spike" and he is like a spiritual son to me.

Just a few weeks ago, I received a surprise letter. It was from Blue Eyes. He said I could share his words:

"I was paroled two years ago. I live in (another city) with my wife and children. God is very active in our lives. I attend church regularly. God cured me of cancer and walked me through the depths of prison life all those years. He sheltered me and guided me to do the right thing. I got my GED and my associate degree while in prison. When I thought I might lose myself again, I locked myself in my cell and prayed or I called my wife and we prayed together. God really answers those prayers. As soon as I was granted parole, God blessed me with a job and gave me a chance to excel in my schooling. I will graduate next May. And I have a beautiful and healthy son who is going to be one in September. God has blessed me and given me another opportunity. I know He has big plans for me."

Blue Eyes went on to say, *"I honestly believe that it was with you where all of this seed was planted. Thank you for your time and the love you and your family gave me."*

Blue Eyes also told me that *Create in Me a Clean Heart* is still his favorite song. He sings his son to sleep with it every night. He ended his note saying, *"I love you, my brother in Christ!"* My brother in Christ – How wonderful to hear those words!

That leaves only one of those young men who had not yet responded. Until now.

"I told the boys, 'I'm going to church.' They looked at each other funny! Then they said 'What?' I said, 'Yeah, I'm goin' to church around the corner!'" That was what Gino said on a recent Friday night.

That was a big deal because he was the most powerful and influential leader on the streets of our community. He has held that position for many years in our part of the South Bronx. He calls me "Pops" and tells everyone on the streets that I am his father, a title that both humbles me and moves my heart with unconditional love for him. He was one of those ordered by that rapper to kill me. They didn't. He stood up to that man and has protected me ever since.

I have prayed for Gino and all of them and loved them unconditionally for over 25 years. This was the first time in his entire life that Gino had been to church.

He walked in with his wife and teenage son. People who knew him -- a lady who lives in the apartment beside his mother and who used to be a drug addict, and a guy who was offered multiple times to join the trade but refused -- walked up to him and hugged him. My son greeted him with a South Bronx "pound" and my daughter wrapped her arms around him with a big hug. Not wanting to make it appear to be the big deal that it was, I simply hugged him and said, "I love you." He responded, "You know I love you more, Pops."

That night was a Family Night at Harvest where the youth and adults sat in the chapel in a big circle of chairs and we talked about family issues and any issues they wanted and needed to share. God led the discussion in a way that it related to everyone and it *really* related to Gino. He and his family were obviously touched.

When the night was over, he talked with several who knew him (everybody knows him) and then he walked outside. I thought he left and decided I would follow up with him later. When I looked outside, he was standing alone on the stoop in front of The Harvest Center. I walked out to join him, but before I did, I realized what he was doing. He was making a statement:

"Hey everyone, look where I am. Look where I have been. I came to church tonight. This church. Harvest Church. I am proud to be here."

That following Sunday, his wife and son gave their hearts to Christ.

And Gino? Well, God is at work in his heart. I have seen this for years. I have seen it in his eyes and felt it in his embrace. I have seen it when he scolded one of his "boys" when he threw a Gospel tract on the ground. He picked it up and told Spike that he keeps them in a drawer and reads them all. By God's grace, He will lift his hands in worship with Christ ruling in his heart, and when he does, our entire community in the South Bronx will be affected by it.

I look back and wonder, what would have happened if I had left when I learned of the threat on my life? Or if I hadn't shown up the day after Blue Eyes warned me? What if I hadn't spoken up at the precinct or if we had reported the abuse before going to Darla's apartment? What if Angel had not smiled and waved at that drug dealer, grabbing that young man's heart? What if I didn't serve them cold soda on the street?

What if, in my weariness and pain, I had quit when breakthrough was around the corner?

God's whispers guide us. His grace is big enough to overcome our failures. His purposes will be fulfilled through us as long as we have surrendered hearts andwe persevere, not relying on our strength and understanding, but on His alone.

He is always pursuing, always loving, and patiently waiting for us to be the living representation of His love and for hurting hearts to open to Him.

He invites us to walk with Him to be a part of His eternal story of hope and light in the darkness.

"I know what I'm doing. I have it all planned out—plans to take care of you, not abandon you, plans to give you the future you hope for. When you call on Me, when you come and pray to Me, I'll listen. When you come looking for Me, you'll find Me" (Jeremiah 29:11-13 The Message Bible).

Chapter Eight

Walking Among the People

"I'll set up my residence in your neighborhood ...
I'll stroll through your streets ...
I am God, your personal God ..."

Leviticus 26:11-13 (The Message Bible)

The Harvest Center was an oasis for the first year. The landlord gave us an apartment upstairs and brought school desks and chairs for us to use for our tutoring program. He also gave us the basement. We renovated it, making the main room a "youth room" and a separate room for a food pantry and clothing closet. Then the basement flooded with raw sewage. We cleaned it up and restocked the food pantry and clothing closet. It flooded again. We cleaned it up again. Then it became infested with rats.

The rat infestation spread from the basement throughout *The Harvest Center*. These were New York City rats, as big as small cats, scurrying around our facility. Sometimes they would run through classes and functions we had, sending women on top of their chairs or out the door screaming. I remember once when three rats ran into the middle of a Bible class and looked at everyone. I told the people that these rats heard the Word, so if they have souls (which of course they do not), they are accountable. After the super of the building put poison in the basement, the rats began to die in the walls and on the drop ceiling. The stench was horrible.

Add to these things financial stress, death threats and the growing opposition of witchcraft, and the pressures against us were very real. But even all these things combined were not as wearisome and heartbreaking as the many souls we met suffering in bondage who did not want to change. It was as if something in them would not allow them to reach forward into freedom. They trusted us, believed us, and loved us, but chose to remain in the pitiful state they were in. Freedom was at their doorstep, but they would not open the door. We could not open it for them.

Abuse was endemic in our neighborhood, both physical and sexual. One 13-year-old girl who was a part of our youth outreach confessed to her mother that she had been sexually abused by her uncles for years. Her mother's response was to throw her out of the home. She went to live with her father, and then her grandmother. The grandmother eventually threw her out on the street, and at 14 years old she ended up in a shelter for teens. But God was still there, even in this situation. She met another young lady in the shelter, hopeless and suicidal, and brought her to Harvest. Today, that young lady is married and involved in missions work. God is a faithful God.

God placed us in reach of suffering people in extreme hopelessness and despair. In a normal week, 80 to 90 percent of the people we were reaching were in crisis situations. It was precisely as Pastor Dave Wilkerson said to me: "Tom, you will not establish a normal church in that community. You will establish a spiritual hospital. Many people will come through your doors. Most you will never hear from again, but what they experience there will change their lives." He was ever so correct.

The daily crises and suffering began to wear on us. We understood why so many inner-city workers either burn out or become hardened to protect their hearts. We had the support and prayers of many, and we leaned hard on Jesus. Those two things, along with the vision God had given us, sustained us and kept us moving forward each day.

After three and a half years, we had a small congregation of about 25 people. We had established after-school tutoring for children and teens, GED tutoring, counseling, and creative arts training. We were very engaged in the community. We fought battles every day for the souls of people.

In the middle of 1998, three and a half years into the establishment of the outreach center, we were weary and brokenhearted. The spiritual warfare was intense, unrelenting and no respecter of persons. I separated myself to pray. I asked God for a strategy that would begin to break the brick walls of oppression that were so prevalent in our community. After about three weeks of prayer, the Lord responded with His direction. It was not anything I would have ever imagined.

"Go to the man who falsely accused you in the first year you were in New York, the man who cut off your support and rejected you. Take a basin and a towel in a paper bag. Go wash his feet and pray for him."

I knew this was not my imagination. I would have never thought of doing something like this. Neither did I understand how this would answer my prayer for our community. But I knew I had to obey, despite my lack of understanding.

I went to the man's office. We spoke casually for a moment. I asked his forgiveness for any way that I may have disrespected him (though truthfully I could think of none). I asked if I could wash his feet and pray for him. He obliged.

As I knelt to untie his shoelaces, a flood of bitterness rose up in my soul. I understood why God had sent me. I had not forgiven him for the things he did against us. As I washed his feet and prayed for him, I forgave him. Peace filled my heart. He never acknowledged his wrong nor asked me to forgive him. That didn't matter. After all, Jesus didn't wait for me to ask for forgiveness. He went to the cross long before I was born and paid with His blood for my forgiveness. Who am I that I would not forgive?

I embraced the man and told him I loved him before I left. It was genuine. God had cleansed me of the unforgiveness that I didn't even recognize in my heart. Freedom came as that burden was lifted. I had done what God wanted me to do. As crazy as it was, I was glad I did. My heart needed to be cleansed of anything and everything that could impede God's plan. Only then could He give the direction I was seeking for our community.

A few days after that experience, the Lord gave His strategy for the Bronx.

"Pray over every household in the community I have sent you. Go door-to-door in groups of two and three. Pray discreetly. Do not knock on the door unless My Spirit leads you."

This was certainly not an idea I would have anticipated or invented on my own. There were more than 350,000 people in a one-mile radius of *The Harvest Center.* The area of Mott Haven God called us to had 80,000 residents. I knew it was God's voice and I was willing to obey.

We enlarged a map of our community and hung it on the wall of our office. We would highlight in yellow each block after we prayed over every household in every building on that block. We began with our building, starting on the top floor and praying discreetly over every household door-to-door, then standing together in the hallway in quiet corporate prayer before going down to the next floor. Our prayers were simple:

God bless this family. Bless these children. If there is any addiction or abuse here, heal it with Your love. Provide for their needs. Help them find the destiny You so lovingly planned for them. Fill this house with Your hope, joy, love and peace . . .

Immediately, things began to happen. The first response came from the people involved in Santeria witchcraft. They made blood and animal sacrifices on the corners of the buildings where we had prayed. It did not deter us. The blood of Jesus Christ is infinitely more powerful.

We had about 25 involved in Harvest at the time. Most of those were under 20 years old. That did not matter. The size or age of our group was not important to Him. After all, His Word says, *"Do not despise these small beginnings, for the Lord rejoices to see the work begin ..."* (Zechariah 4:10). What was important to God was *obedience.*

God responded to that obedience by doing two profound and powerful things: God built the faith of our people. They began to believe His Word for what it says. *"You can say to this mountain, 'May you be lifted up and thrown into the sea,' and it will happen"* (Mark 11:23). We were facing mountains of fear, despair, hopelessness, addiction, violence, abuse, poverty, neglect, and so much more entrenched generation across generation in this community. We knew human efforts had failed to make a difference for generations. We grew to understand that if we prayed, the community not only could change, it *would* change.

Many times we would walk out the door to prayerwalk and I would watch our faithful followers of Christ look at the soles of their shoes and personalize the promise given to Moses and Joshua, *"The land upon which we set our feet today will belong to You, Lord!"* God was building the faith of His people at Harvest as we prayed over the community, and this would have a great impact going forward.

The second profound and powerful thing God did was through divine appointments. Every day that we prayerwalked, God placed someone in our path who needed a prayer, an encouraging word, a ray of hope in the dark place of despair. It was as if people were waiting for us every time we went out to prayerwalk! Over and over, we met people hungry for something real, something genuine and authentic, something that would really touch the painful depth of their need, and we had it. We had Jesus, and He would make the difference. All God needed was for us to get out the doors into the streets to meet them face-to-face with His grace.

We walked and prayed. Rain or shine. Summer hot or winter cold. Many times, we waited in the rain or frigid weather for someone leaving an apartment building to open the door so that we could enter and pray.

The more we prayerwalked, the more God taught us. Jesus said, *"For where two or three gather together in My name, I am there among them"* (Matthew 18:20). We were bringing the presence of Jesus Christ into communities of darkness and spiritual bondage. Since it is His presence that changes things, this is precisely what was (and still is) needed . . . *His* presence, manifested through the lives of His loving children.

Worshipping God outdoors became a particularly important part of announcing the truth of God's love, proclaiming hope, and taking back the streets. The scripture teaches us that the Spirit of Christ literally inhabits the praises of His people. He doesn't just look down on it; *He sits down in the middle of it and stays there when He is desired and made welcome.* One thing is for sure, the bondage that we witnessed every day was not just flesh and blood from earth. Paul the Apostle said, *"For we are not fighting against flesh-and-blood enemies, but against evil rulers and authorities of the unseen world, ... against evil spirits in heavenly places"* (Ephesians 6:12). Paul said in 2 Corinthians 10:3-4 (NASB), *"For though we walk in the flesh, we do not war according to the flesh, for the weapons of our warfare are not of the flesh, but divinely powerful for the destruction of fortresses."* We needed weapons that were divinely powerful for the destruction of strongholds. Prayer and worship in the places of darkness became and have remained two of the most powerful weapons God has given us.

I have often wondered; what warfare takes place in the heavenlies when we worship in places of spiritual darkness? Do armies of angels invade the throne rooms of rulers and authorities of darkness and declare, "The church of the Living Christ is here! Move out of the way, for Jesus has given us the keys to your gates. God's people are worshipping in Spirit and in Truth, and we have come to take back what you have stolen!"

All of this was birthed through a simple yet miraculous way to bring hope into areas of darkness and oppression: praying with people door-to-door and prayerwalking the streets and public places.

As people came to the door, I would say, "Hello! I'm Tom Grassano. I'm not here to preach at you. I'm not here to invite you to church. I don't have any materials to give you. The only reason I am here is that God told us to pray for every family on this block. May I ask, what is your name, and how we can pray for you?" Person after person broke into tears. Many invited us in, calling their family into the room for us to pray with them. Many are in churches today as a result. In one of the most amazing miracles I have ever experienced, every time that I have prayerwalked since God spoke to me in 1998, whether in the South Bronx, Detroit, other American cities, Cuba, the favelas of Brazil, cities and villages in Southeast Asia or elsewhere, I have met someone set up by God's divine appointment to bring hope into his/her life. I believe it will always be that way.

God's Spirit prompted me one day to search the Gospels and see how many miracles of Jesus took place in the synagogues. My eyes were opened. Of all the miracles of Jesus recorded in the Gospels, only three took place in the synagogues. All the rest took place as He was walking among the people. I just can't find the scripture to tell us to do it any differently today!

God transformed my understanding of His calling upon my life. God did not call me to plant and pastor a church. He called me to pastor the streets around us. He called me to pastor a community! He did not want us to reinvent and implement ministry methods and strategies to bring people to our doors. *He wanted us to bring Jesus to their doorsteps, with love and hope, in a heart-language they could understand!* This remains the mission of our ministry today.

We prayerwalked for three and a half years. That was how long it took for us tofinish praying over every household in our community, going out two to four times a week. I still stand amazed that we began prayerwalking three-and-a-half years into our ministry there and finished three-and-a-half years later, seven years into our ministry in the South Bronx.

I vividly remember the day Jeff Wilson took a highlighter and colored in the final block on our map of our community. We had accomplished what God instructed us to do, praying over every household in our community.

Then we did one final thing: we prayerwalked around the entire South Bronx. We split into two groups. We began at *The Harvest Center* and walked to the bottom of Brook Avenue, praying as we went. One group turned to the west and walked up the Grand Concourse to the Courthouse, and then across 161st Street to the top of Brook Avenue. My group turned to the east and proceeded up the Bruckner to Hunts Point, and then across 161st to Brook Avenue.

Our plan was to meet at *The Harvest Center,* but in divine providence we turned the corner and both groups met at the top of Brook Avenue. We walked back together from 161st to 148th, singing praises through the streets. When we arrived, something prompted me to count the people who prayerwalked that day. There were exactly 120, just like the Upper Room.

We were finished. We had completed what God instructed us to do, but God had just begun. That was when miracles happened, and change came to our community.

It began with our precinct. A precinct well known for corruption was cleaned up. Multiple cops in our precinct, the 40th, and the 30th precinct in Washington Heights, were indicted. As a result, a new crop of police with integrity came in, which included two Captains and several police who were followers of Jesus Christ and were seeking the best for our community.

Drugs and gangs were cleaned out of the parks and playgrounds. Children began to play on the streets and in playgrounds once controlled by drug dealers. The violent crime rate, once one of the highest in New York City and the nation, decreased. Children and youth programs started, helping kids stay in school and decreasing illiteracy. (Ours was the only after-school program in our immediate area for years.) Slumlord apartments were torn down and new two- and three-family homes were built in their place. Families purchased these homes at low down payments and rented one or two floors to pay their mortgage. Unemployment decreased. New businesses came into the community. Many of the young drug dealers began to change. They began working jobs, marrying their girlfriends, learning to be respectable fathers, and some began serving Christ.

What were the results of all these things? Dignity returned to families, and hope, along with its companion peace, came to our community.

A community that once considered the church irrelevant opened its arms to us. Organizations like the Police Athletic League and housing project tenants' associations invited us to do children's outreach at their functions, giving us the freedom to share eternal hope with children and their parents. The school district co-sponsored three worship concert events in a junior high school auditorium, writing to the PTA of all surrounding schools encouraging people to come. The Community Board supported and affirmed our programs. I was invited to speak for Career Day at South Bronx High School for six years and at the Symposium for Equality and Justice in Manhattan schools for three years.

And while all of these miraculous advances may not be the direct result of UHM programs, we believe they are a direct result of God raising up a body of believers who, no longer living as victims, are pursuing their destinies with joy and freedom, seeking to honor Christ in their daily lives and choices, living out their faith and believing God when they pray.

I believe the transformation can be summed up in this way: God called us to do something that seemed a bit strange at first, but we obeyed. We persevered for three and a half years. God looked down and saw a remnant of His possession faithfully doing as He instructed us to do, and He shined His favor down, poking a hole in the dark cloud of oppression in our community. *His favor changed things.*

As a result, God "set up shop" in Fort Apache, the South Bronx.

The Gospel, if allowed by the church, will powerfully affect lives. If our faith possesses a radical commitment of all that we are to all that He is in every part of our lives, the Gospel will permeate every part of the human being to the very core – as the Word says, to the marrow of our being (Hebrews 4:12), and thus to the very core of our homes, our families, our churches, our communities, and even our nation.

If the Gospel is not allowed to radically and dramatically transform our ways of thinking and our ways of doing, if instead we are busy going through the motions of religion, if we are content with a small taste of heaven that affects our emotions rather than changing our lifestyles and transforming our thinking, then we are subjecting ourselves to an impotent and irrelevant faith. We will continue living in mediocrity without transformational change. Our communities will remain the same, and pastors will continue moving from one church problem to another rather than being challenged by the vision that God has given for the harvest fields of the communities around us.

We need the presence of Christ where strongholds of darkness have been free to keep people in bondage for generations. That will happen when God's people put love into action and walk among the people like Jesus did.

We have all most likely heard the expression, *Prayer changes things.* I believe that prayer does change things, but it changes us first and then shows us how we can be a part of the answer. The question really is, *are we willing to approach God with hunger and thirst that cannot be satisfied with anything but Jesus and complete abandon to God's ways?*

The depth of crises and suffering I have encountered in the inner city and two- thirds world have brought me to the end of myself over and over. *"What can I really do to help? How can I make a difference?"* were the questions I repeatedly asked. All my ideas fell short in truly answering the deepest-of-the-heart questions others were asking. Eventually, after God took His chisel and chipped away at my understanding and at my heart, He left me with three things: *love them, pray for them, and tell them the Truth of God's love.*

I learned that praying for them meant not only talking to God about them and about how to help them but talking to God about how I needed to change to become a better agent of change. Coming to the end of myself, not just once but many times, made me not run away but run closer to the cross. What happens when you get closer to the cross? You die more to yourself, and Jesus lives more in you.

I heard someone say that one of the greatest reasons we as a church are not consumed by the Great Commission is because we are not broken. I believe there is a lot of truth in that. Pride, fear and personal agendas get in the way. Prayer in desperation leads us to know the things about ourselves we don't often want to know. Thankfully, that leads us to the One who knew them anyway, loves us anyway, and opens the door to transform us so that His mercy can flow with greater impact in us and through us.

Prayer certainly changes things, but it changes us first.

Some years ago, a young teenager visiting us with a mission team from Rincon, Georgia, shared a scripture that she said reminded her of our community and the transformation that was taking place among and around us. It is from Revelation 21:3 in The Message Bible -

"I heard a voice thunder from the Throne: "Look! Look! God has moved into the neighborhood, making His home with men and women!"

God moved into our neighborhood, and the neighborhood will never be the same.

Chapter Nine

A Wedding, a Funeral, and a Casket Factory

"The Lord directs our steps."

Proverbs 20:24

The phone rang in my office. "Hello?"

"Hello, Pastor Tom! It's Manny!"

I knew dozens of Manny's in the South Bronx. I wondered, "Which one is this?"

"You remember me? Manny! I used to sell drugs in your building!"

Of course, I remembered *that* Manny!

Manny and I began to talk. It had been a while and it was so good to hear his voice. I never forgot one thing about Manny. A lady addicted to cocaine came to *The Harvest Center* for help. She responded and spent a month clean until she received her next check from the government. She went straight to Manny to buy cocaine, but he would not sell it to her. He told her, "I've seen that Pastor Tom is trying to help you. I will not disrespect him by selling to you. Go back to him and let him help you or get your drugs somewhere else." She came back and told me what Manny had said.

Manny continued, "I'm getting married!" He told me about his fiancé, how they met, what they wanted for their wedding, and more. I was so blessed that he wanted to inform me about this part of his life! Then Manny said, "I want my pastor to marry me!" I began to rejoice that he was in a church somewhere, until Manny said, "You don't get it, do you? You're my pastor. You're the only pastor I've ever had."

By loving people in the South Bronx, Lidia and I became adopted parents to many of the children and youth on the streets. I had also become the pastor of the community. This resulted in the people coming to us with their crises, joys, pains, and yes, weddings and funerals.

Manny and I began to talk about the wedding. I informed him the only way I would perform the wedding was for him and his fiancé to meet with me every week until the wedding. They did, and on the third meeting, they opened their hearts to faith in Christ.

The wedding day came. Decorations were beautiful. We were all excited. A lady walked in the door with Godzilla-sized rollers in her hair, a tank top, pajama bottoms and flip flops. We asked her if she would like to use the bathroom to change. She said, "Oh no, I'm fine." Sure enough, that was her attire for the wedding.

The Harvest Center filled up with drug dealers, former drug dealers, drug addicts, former drug addicts, and a transvestite with his boyfriend. He was the cousin of the bride. He wanted to be in the wedding party. She told him he could if he came as a guy. He refused. Some of the guests were dressed in suits, some in South Bronx street clothes, and one in Godzilla-sized hair rollers with a tank top, pajama bottoms and flip flops.

This event was a beautiful example of our ministry. God had opened the doors for us to reach everyone in our community. It didn't matter what they looked like, how they dressed, what they smelled like, what their habits were, or anything else. All are created in God's image. All are accepted by Him. He doesn't require us to change before we walk in the doors, but He won't leave us the same if we come to Him with an open heart.

As had become my custom, I began the wedding with an exhortation about the Author of Love and what His love is like – unconditional, kind and gentle, not keeping a list of our wrongs, patient, never demanding or self-seeking, hoping for the best in all circumstances, a love demonstrated most of all by the gift of His Son. I shared about Jesus and what His love can do in our lives. I gave the opportunity for anyone to respond to His love, and many did.

The wedding was followed by a funeral a few weeks later. A woman who infrequently worshipped with us called me. Her nephew had died. He was 43 years old. He had just gotten out of jail, mugged a doctor in the parking lot of Kings County Hospital in Brooklyn and stole his BMW. His joy ride resulted in a police chase which ended with him crashing into the side of a project building, dying instantly.

The family had no one to officiate the funeral. The aunt recommended me, and the family asked her to contact me. I accepted, and I prayed.

I have participated in too many funerals in the Bronx. Too many people dying too early from tragic circumstances that make funerals very dark and oppressive, especially for families who have been in that situation too many times before.

I arrived at the funeral home in Brooklyn, met the funeral home director and then proceeded into the chapel to meet the family. As I found my seat, I heard an awful commotion in the back of the chapel. A fight had broken out between two of the brothers of the deceased. Police rushed in and broke up the fight. Six police officers then positioned themselves in the chapel to keep the peace.

I noticed I was the only man with light skin in the place. At Harvest, there is no color. There is no Black or White or Hispanic or anything else. We are one in Christ and we are all family. But this funeral was not Harvest.

The first two-and-a-half rows of the funeral home chapel were filled with men wearing turbans. The deceased was an adherent of the Nation of Islam, as were his friends. With the fight and the presence of these friends, I realized what I had prepared to share was not appropriate for this day. Then something happened that unequivocally convinced me I needed to change gears in my remarks.

When the funeral service was about to begin, the mother of the deceased stood up, turned around facing the people, lifted her finger and said, "If anyone, *anyone,* says one good thing about my son, I will curse you out."

Okay! What next?! I had been in many situations that took me far out of my comfort zone and forced me to lean heavy on God's grace and guidance. This funeral was near the top of that list.

The funeral service began with a relative standing up and reading the obituary. He sat down. It was my turn.

I slowly stood up, leaving all my notes on the pew. Pleading with God for His mercy, I walked to the front.

God gave me His words.

"First of all, many of you have judged me by the color of my skin and you don't even know me. So, let me tell you who I am."

God gave me their attention with that statement. I briefly shared our story about how God had brought us to the South Bronx and what He called us to do.

Then I spoke the words God had given me. I pointed to the casket and said, "You see in this casket a son, a brother, an uncle, a cousin, a grandson, a friend. What I see is a life of regret. When I look at you, I see many lives of regret. Let me tell you how to live life with no regret."

I proceeded to share about a guy who was born into an adulterous relationship with his mother and father. During the first twelve years of his life, his family experienced murder, rape, incest, rebellion, homelessness and more murder. His father was named David. His mother was named Bathsheba. His parents named him Solomon, but when the prophet Nathan walked into the room to meet the baby, he said, "God will call him Jedidiah" (2 Samuel 12:25).

Jedidiah means *loved by God.* Despite the dysfunction of his family, God loved him and had created him with a destiny.

The same is true for all of us.

I shared how God had created each one of them with a unique destiny and how this pathway can lead to life with no regret. Then I did something I had never done before at a funeral. I opened the door for anyone there to begin a new life with Jesus Christ.

Five people raised their hands to do so.

I concluded with prayer. The funeral was done. The family came forward to grieve one last time at the coffin.

I slipped out the back door of the chapel and into the bathroom, standing in bewilderment at where God had placed me and what He had just done. Then the door of the bathroom opened. An older man walked in, came straight to me, embraced me and wept on my shoulder. The man said, "You don't know me. I am the father of the deceased. Do you know what my other sons and their friends are doing right now? They are standing outside talking about all that you said to them. Thank you for speaking into the lives of my family. Thank you for what you did today." He shook my hand and walked out the door.

I don't know what God did with the seeds sown that day, but I do remember what God showed me from Isaiah 55 when Hector walked up to me at Way Out Ministries my first day in the Bronx: *"So will My word be which goes forth from My mouth; It will not return to Me empty, without accomplishing what I desire, and without succeeding in the matter for which I sent it" (Isaiah 55:11 NASB).*

The funeral of a criminal that erupted into a fight among family members resulted in sharing about hope and eternal life. God uses seemingly inopportune times to share His grace if we let Him.

We spent five years in *The Harvest Center.* The first year was a blessing enjoying our first facility in the community, but we rapidly outgrew the 700-square-feet space. Creative scheduling had different age groups present at different times. The next four years were filled with rat infestation, water damage from bathrooms above us, and no heat in the wintertime. The lack of heat did not deter people from coming. *The Harvest Center* was a place of life, hope, joy, and peace. It was safe. It was filled with unconditional love. We would huddle around space heaters during our programs.

We began crying out to God for a new place. We looked at several facilities, but none felt right. Across the street was the abandoned coffin factory used by drug dealers, homeless drug addicts, and gangsters. It was the same building I was looking at when God spoke to me years before and said, *"Prepare yourself, Tom; I have future ministry for you here."* We had prayed over this building since our first trip in 1992, often walking around it and laying hands on it in prayer. We felt God wanted to do something special there, something with supernatural purpose. We could not let that feeling go.

Someone started renovating the building. The abandoned factory was in such disrepair that when they began renovations, the roof fell five floors to the basement. I researched who was supervising this renovation, what they would be doing with the building, and if rental of part of it would be possible. I learned that SoBro oversaw the renovations. SoBro is an organization in the South Bronx offering employment assistance, entrepreneurial development and business assistance. I called and set up a meeting to present ourselves and share our need for space for our programs.

Jeff Wilson, the young man who joined me in 1996 for a summer internship, stayed for six years. He was one of the greatest servants I have ever worked with. Jeff went with me to the meeting at SoBro. The receptionist brought us into the office of the vice-president. After introductions, I began to share about Urban Harvest and our work in the community. I shared about our need for space and how interested we were to lease in their building.

"We are impressed by all that you are doing, but this building is being renovated with federal funding. Sorry, separation of church and state. We can't lease to your organization."

I left heartbroken. What would we do? This was our dream! We left the office with disappointment.

Early the next morning, my phone rang. "Dr. Grassano, this is Neil, vice-president of SoBro."

"Yes, Neil. How can I help you?"

"We need to know what we need to do to get you into our building."

I was shocked to hear those words after the meeting we had the previous day. They were asking $35 a square foot to lease with the lessee being responsible for all the renovations of the space. Without hesitation, I said, "You need to lower the rent."

"How much?" Neil asked. Off the top of my head, I said, "$13 a square foot." Neil said, "Okay."

I was amazed! I was also upset at myself that I didn't say $6 a square foot!

Neil said, "Come in and let's sign the lease!"

I learned later from another SoBro employee that Neil had called the Chairman of our Community Board who told him, "We cannot lose this organization from our community! Do whatever you need to do to give them space and keep them in Mott Haven."

Thank You, God, for Your favor.

Jeff and I walked to the SoBro office the next day and signed the lease. Walking back to *The Harvest Center* down East 148th Street, I began to feel very mixed emotions. We had a new base for outreach, but we had literally no funds to begin the renovations or for the increase in rent. I remember saying to myself, *"Oh God, what did I just do?"*

I was reminded that day of something that happened when I was a child in Detroit. My father's church had outgrown their facility. They desperately needed to build a new church. As they were looking around, they found a property they fell in love with and, in prayer, believed this was God's location for the new church, but it was already under contract.

One cold October evening after dinner, my father told me to get my coat. We were going for a ride. He drove my mother and I to the property. We walked to the middle of this open field. Mom and Dad took a Bible, laid it on the ground and asked God for that property. What I recall most of all was that a six-year-old boy in the middle of a field would normally be running all over the place. Instead, there was a presence of God that kept me standing right there while they prayed.

The next day, the realtor called and informed my father that the organization that had the property under contract pulled out. He could have it if he wanted it. The church purchased the property and began building the church. They broke ground with steel girders on the ground and little funding to continue. Dad read scripture, made some remarks and prayed. Dad and some of the elders took their shovels and broke ground. Then Dad turned to the choir director and asked the choir to sing a song,

We've come this far by faith, leaning on the Lord, Trusting in His holy Word; He's never failed us yet! Oh, we can't turn around! We've come this far by faith!

The same God who was God of my father's ministry, my grandfather's ministry, and my father-in-law's ministry, who provided and saw all of them through every challenging situation, would be God of our ministry and would come through for us.

We had a group of men from the Landmark Church of God in Statesville, North Carolina scheduled to begin our renovations. On a Monday in October 2000, two weeks before their arrival, I printed our financials and spread them out on my desk. I took a calculator and found that, without completing renovations and with the increase in rent, we could remain open until June 2001. I looked up at the Lord, and said, "If that is Your plan, You will give us somewhere else to go."

The next day, Harold Downing, a minister from South Carolina called me. After greeting me, he said something I had never heard before or since, "Tom, are you sitting down? You might want to be."

He informed me that the council of the Church of God in South Carolina had met the previous day. A member of the council, Pastor Bobby Johnson of Praise Cathedral in Greer, gave them a challenge. Pastor Johnson had visited us on a weekend about two months before. We walked around the community. I showed him the casket factory and shared the vision of what we wanted to do. He ministered on Sunday and left. It was a nice visit, but that seemed to be it.

Harold Downing continued speaking, "Pastor Johnson challenged us today. He informed us that his church is donating $10,000 to your ministry to help with your renovations and he challenged us to match it. Then he reminded us of the amount we have sitting in savings doing nothing. He challenged us, saying, "If we are a ministry, why is money sitting in the bank that could be used for ministry?"

"Tom, God moved on us. We decided to give away $100,000 to seven ministry organizations, and yours is one of them."

The council then approached the Children of the World Foundation to match the grant, which they did. God had provided!

But for us, God had not just provided for a new place, *He provided for a new home on the same block where He had called me eight years before!* He provided for a new home in an abandoned casket factory, bringing life in a community of death in a renovated casket factory.

God's words to me in 1992, *"Prepare yourself, Tom, I have future ministry for you here,"* did not just mean in the South Bronx in New York City, He meant *on this block!*

The renovations took several months. God gave me the layout and colors for everything almost like a vision. The new *Harvest Center* had a large classroom that could be divided into two rooms on the right side of the entranceway and a beautiful chapel on the left. On a large wall 18 feet wide is a mural painted with children of all nations praying. Underneath the painting are the words, *"My house will be a house of prayer for all nations."* On the other side of the mural, a large cross is hanging on the wall, about eight feet tall, stained to a cherry and mahogany tone. I made it myself.

Half of the floor is wood floor, provided by the owners of the building. The chapel itself has a dark cherry wood floor. One day the contractor of the rest of the building came by and asked what we wanted for the floor of the chapel. He provided it to the tune of $10,000. When it was done, he looked at it and said with a smile, "It's perfect."

Scriptures and promises of God were written on all the sheetrock and floors before walls were painted and carpet was laid. Those whose lives had been changed were assigned to do this along with us and our staff. Isaiah 61:1-3, part of our vision statement, and Galatians 2:20, my personal mission statement, were placed where the pulpit would be. We spent that evening rejoicing over all that God had done and all that He was about to do.

I stained and installed shutters in the large windows of the chapel and entranceway. A Native American artist from Alaska, whom I had met years before, made a cross to hang behind the pulpit on the stage. Pastor Ken Hudson from Landmark Church of God in North Carolina, where the men who began the renovations worship, donated the pulpit. Lidia placed a table with candles in the entranceway and beautiful curtains over the windows on each side of the main door. The eyes of every visitor lit up with joy when they opened the door.

We constructed a library/conference room and offices downstairs. We installed bookshelves around areas where they used to store caskets. We installed desks in the staff office and my office that were made to fit the space. Through the miraculous provision, we purchased computers, classroom materials for the children's outreach and tutoring programs, and a new ministry van. It was everything we had dreamed of.

We finished the three-and-a-half years of prayerwalking the community at the same time we finished the renovations. We dedicated the building on April 7, 2001, Palm Sunday, exactly five years after we dedicated the first *Harvest Center*. The dedication was beautiful. The chapel was filled to capacity with people from our community, from other churches in the Bronx, and from the leadership of Urban Harvest Ministries. We shared about how our glory is in the Cross, giving thanks to all who made this possible, especially the One to whom it is all dedicated. My father challenged us about our mission and gave the dedicatory prayer. Our theme scripture for the dedication was,

"My eyes will be open and My ears attentive to every prayer made in this place. For I have chosen this Temple and set it apart to be holy—a place where My name will be honored forever. I will always watch over it, for it is dear to My heart" (2 Chronicles 7:15-16).

By this time, the miracles from the prayerwalking were already taking place. Our ministry vision didn't change, but the responsiveness of people did. Outreach was in full swing – prayerwalking, after-school tutoring, youth outreach, children's outreach, block parties, outdoor worship concerts, Prayer Stations and more.

At one Prayer Station (a table on the street where we offer prayer with people along with free Bibles and scripture booklets), a young man came to one of my leaders and said, "Hey lady, do you remember me? You prayed for me before!" As they engaged in conversation, the young man said, "I asked you to pray for me to get a job, but you prayed for my protection. Two weeks later I was shot four times. The doctors said I should have died. I knew I didn't because you prayed that prayer!" She shared with him the plans God has for him and he opened his heart to Jesus.

On another occasion, a lady came to our Prayer Station asking for prayer for a job. We prayed for God to answer that prayer. Fifteen minutes later, she came back with a miracle story. "After you prayed with me, I went into that store across the street to buy some things. They had a help wanted sign on the counter. I asked about it, and now I have a job! God answered your prayer!" I almost responded saying, "Lady, it's not supposed to happen that fast!"

Another time at a Prayer Station, a man walked by in a hurry. One of our youth offered to pray for him. He reluctantly obliged. Over an hour later, he came back and told us a miraculous story. He was hired to kill someone. He was on his way to do it when we prayed with him. After that prayer, he proceeded to complete his task, but he couldn't do it. He threw his gun away and came back to the Prayer Station. He and I talked over pizza for an hour and a half. He left in peace with himself and God.

These things did not happen without opposition. Those involved in witchcraft increased their activity against us. For 16 straight months, every time we came to the new *Harvest Center* there were sacrifices on our doorstep. One evening, one of my workers found four witches outside our door casting curses against our facility and us. Then something divinely profound happened.

A major snowstorm hit New York City. It shut down bus service and delayed subway service, limiting the amount of people who could get to church on Sunday. That didn't stop worship at Harvest. Our people worshipped with all their hearts.

One young adult described our worship this way once, referring to the scripture, *"Those who have been forgiven much, love much, and they worship much!"* On this particular Sunday, we spent more than an hour just singing in joyful worship after church. We didn't know that two Santeria followers were standing outside in the snow watching.

The next day, one of them was walking past our facility and one of our young adults greeted her. She told him she had watched us worshipping the previous day. He asked why she didn't come in. She responded, "We were afraid!"

We followed up with her and her sister. Both threw their idols and Santeria materials into an incinerator and burned them. *To God be the glory!*

We were so thrilled with our new facility that multiple floods of raw sewage did not deter us from our mission. Desks, computers, books, files, and furniture were damaged, but we pressed on. There were times that flooding would start while ministry programs were in full swing. We immediately suspended programs and all ages moved into action forming a chain as we passed pails of sewer water up the stairs, out the front door and into the drains in the street. We often did this singing worship unto the Lord. These things only drew us closer together and made us more determined to complete the mission God had begun.

To this day, I stand amazed at the plans of Almighty God. It was not enough for him to place us in one of the most notorious buildings in the community. He also placed us in the building I was looking at when God called me there. Now I fully understood His call to me, *"Prepare yourself, Tom; I have future ministry for you here."* Right here, on this block.

"For I know the plans I have for you," says the LORD. "They are plans for good and not for disaster, to give you a future and a hope. In those days when you pray, I will listen. If you look for Me wholeheartedly, you will find Me. I will be found by you," says the LORD" (Jeremiah 29:11-13).

Chapter Ten

Putting Good Back into Benevolence

"Suppose you see a brother or sister who has no food or clothing, and you say, 'Good-bye and have a good day; stay warm and eat well,' but then you don't give that person any food or clothing. What good does that do?"

James 2:15-16

"Don't pity us."

That was what a South Bronx teen said to an international leader of a denomination who was visiting us with his family. After those from the South Bronx shared their hearts about ministry in their community and the authentic needs of the people (what they needed and what they didn't need), I gave a teenager the opportunity to have the final words. This was the same teen who was in a shelter at 14 years old. I called her name and said, "You will have the last word today. What thought would you like to leave with Dr. Hill?"

She took only a few seconds to think, scooted to the edge of her chair, leaned forward and, with a somber sincerity said, *"Don't pity us. Pastor Tom and Sister Lidia didn't pity us. They gave us tough love. They treated us with dignity. They loved us unconditionally. They helped us stand on our own feet. They didn't feel sorry for us. So don't pity us."*

Did you know that one of the synonyms of pity is *shame* and that the word is designed to be used to express *regret?* Pity really communicates, "I *regret* that you are who you are. I *regret* you live in the condition you live in. I *regret* that you have that family. I *regret* that you live in those projects and go to that school. I *regret* that you have limited opportunity. What a *shame.* I feel *sorry* for you."

That is precisely the package that wraps much benevolence, and it has a *pitiful* stench to it. It is not saying, "I believe in you. I know you have a destiny. I know with God you can overcome anything. I know you have the ability. I know you have the talent. I know you have the intelligence. I know you can rise above anything. I know you will succeed. Yes, it will take hard work and commitment, but God will be with you each step of the way, and so will I. I believe in you!"

That's not pity. That's *vision. Purpose. Strength.* That produces *joy.* That wakes you up in the morning, makes you look up at God and say, *"With You, I can do anything!"*

Much of what we call benevolence does not come in that package. Far too often, it comes in a package prepared to bless the giver more than the receiver, or it comes with a stubborn-headed pride that imposes its way with no regard whatsoever for what the people really feel, think or even what they really need.

We have annual block parties. We often do one as an end-of-school / beginning-of-summer bash when we launch our summer outreach season. In 2003, I was contacted by an international ministry who wanted to bring a semi-truck full of "quality items" (so they said) that could be distributed at our block party. "Take only what you need!" were the words of the director. We spoke about what they were bringing. When he said school supplies, I lit up! That was what we needed most.

They arrived that day in the semi and an SUV with truck drivers, staff, leadership of that ministry, and a videographer with high-tech video equipment.

We are careful using cameras. We have had people from our community leave events when visiting volunteers pulled out cameras. We explained that to these visitors and they promised to be discreet. Despite our continual promptings, the cameraman was very visible during the entire event. Ignoring our objections, the staff opened the back of the truck and began to distribute their goods. Finally, after appealing to the director, they closed the back of the truck and people refocused on the activities of the block party.

After a few hours, the leaders came to me, thanked me for hosting them, and told me they had to leave. The director reminded me to take *"only what you need."*

When the block party finished, the staff with the truck came and asked me where to unload the remainder of the materials in the truck. I informed them of my conversation with their director and told them that we would only take the school supplies. Red in the face with anger, one of them raised his voice and said, "We are unloading all of this cargo even if we have to leave it on the sidewalk!"

And they did.

We filled *The Harvest Center* with non-perishable food items until our classroom space was full. We had barely enough room to walk in the hallways. Then the truck staff kept their promise. With no more room in our facility, they left a couple pallets of expired, generic cereal boxes on the sidewalk.

I stood in the window watching people from our community, whom we did not know, fight over boxes of expired generic cereal. I was heartbroken. "Lord," I prayed, "I will never allow Your name to be disgraced this way again!"

We inventoried the supplies we were given and got a dumpster (not a cheap thing to do in New York City) to dispose of two-thirds of the supplies because they were expired and crushed. A couple of months later we were invited to a large youth event in another state co-sponsored by the organization that sent the truck. They unveiled a video sharing their new urban emphasis. More than 90 percent of the video was footage from our ministry and block party, claiming it as their ministry event. People at the youth conference came to me afterward saying, "We didn't know you were under that ministry!" We were not.

When I was a teenager, I fell in love with the song *Takin' It to the Streets* by The Doobie Brothers. I learned to play it on the piano and sang it all the time. It took me years, however, to understand part of the lyrics:

"You, tellin' me the things you're gonna do for me,
I ain't blind and I don't like what I think I see ... "

Amen to that.

This is an example of benevolence that hurts more than it helps. It divides rather than builds bridges. It disregards the people working in the communities who have forged relationships of trust through blood, sweat, many, many tears and years of story among the people. It is a prideful, self-centered *"We know best what you need"* attitude that relieves the guilt of the giver and gives them a false sense of doing something that matters. In most circumstances, it doesn't. In many cases, it only hurts.

Why not throw our junk there – the clothes we don't wear anymore, the food we don't want to eat anyway, and the toys our kids don't play with anymore? Why not give our second-hand stuff to the people we *pity*? It makes us feel good! Don't they need that stuff in the *ghetto* anyway?

The word *ghetto* evokes many emotions. For some, it evokes fear. Images of gangbangers and drug dealers controlling the streets, perpetuated by Hollywood and hip-hop producers who glamorize and profiteer the urban streets people call home. It suggests visions of poverty, sub-standard housing, disenfranchised people, neglected children, and abandoned buildings with human residents living where no one should live in this land of unequal opportunity. It generates thoughts of people crowded together, scared, angry, out to get any outsider who drifts into their turf.

For many on the outside looking in, that's what *ghetto* means.

Dictionaries define *ghetto* as "a section of a city, a thickly populated slum area, inhabited predominantly by members of an ethnic or other minority group, often as a result of social or economic restrictions, pressures, or hardships"(www.dictionary.com). History tells us that the word originated in the early 1600s and was the name of an island near Venice where Jews were forced to live in exile, trapped in isolation and robbed of human dignity and opportunity.

Sounds quite like the ghettos in our world today – trapped, limited opportunity, people with no sense of destiny and no hope for the future.

The word *ghetto* has Italian origins, derived from the word *ghettare* which means *to throw.* In today's terms, it would mean *to throw away,* because that was what many people, institutions and organizations have done with the precious people from *the ghetto.*

Few communities in our nation better reflect the stereotype of *ghetto* than Fort Apache, the South Bronx. That's what some New Yorkers call our South Bronx community - *the ghetto.*

Headlines from our community over recent years are heart-breaking:

- Seven-year-old girl dies from stray gunfire at a July 4 party. (She was part of our children's program.)
- Girl shot at her 12th birthday party by gang members.
- Six-month old "falls" out of third story project window.
- Six-year-old body found in project dumpster. (He was beaten to death by his mother's boyfriend and then left in a garbage bag in the apartment for almost a week before being disposed of.)
- 13-year-old held as a sex slave in basement by building super for over a year.

For those living in Fort Apache, this is home. The sights and sounds are home. The emotions here are real. The anger is real. The hurt and despair are very, *very* real.

Statistics mean nothing. Living from one day to the next means something. Trying to get an education in sub-standard schools means something. Getting a job and a decent place to live means something. Raising your children . . . or grandchildren . . . and protecting them from the evil on the streets *means something*.

People in the *ghetto* don't need band aids, handouts or pity. They need a real, touchable God whose awesome unconditional love can heal and transform their lives. They find that love through the authenticity and consistency of relationships we build with them.

Love breaks down walls. It is the flavor of life that makes the difference. It brings the aroma of Christ into the stench of hopelessness and death. It makes people willing to listen because they know that they are loved and they are safe in a relationship with us.

As I stood in a window of *The Harvest Center* watching people fight over expired generic cereal boxes on our sidewalk, I made a promise to God: I would never allow His name to be disgraced in that way again.

I kept my promise.

I researched benevolence. The word has Latin roots. *"Bene"* means *good* or *well.* Benevolence is defined as seeking the good and well-being of people.

Are we really doing that with our forms of benevolence?

I called our staff and leaders together and shared my heart with them. Some of them were social workers. Some of them used to be addicted. Some of them were abused. All of them were being discipled in the environment that the teenager described to the denominational leader:

"Pastor Tom and Sister Lidia didn't pity us. They gave us tough love. They treated us with dignity. They loved us unconditionally. They helped us stand on our own feet. They didn't feel sorry for us."

I shared with our leaders about who we as an organization need to be in reaching the needs of people. We discussed this in detail.

We searched the Bible for precedents on what we stereotypically call benevolence. What we learned opened our eyes and indicted the church for throwing our things at people, robbing them of their dignity, enabling them to remain where they are, building no relationship with them, never hearing their story or knowing their pain.

We took a month to pray and fast and set a date to come back together. The result is what we call our *Ministry of Care.* Here is how it works:

Step 1 We become acquainted with people's needs because of our relationships in the community and our outreach ministries. We meet people through outreach. We meet parents of children in our programs. We learn about needs from neighbors and friends. We pray for God to lead us to those we can help, and He does.

Step 2 Once we encounter the need, we meet with the individual, couple, or parent. Many of our leaders have lived and understand how life can do these things to people, so they conduct these meetings. Their stories help them relate to the people. Through a very informal interview lavished with love, we encounter what brought this individual or family to this place of need.

Step 3 Once we know the journey that brought them to this place, we prayerfully formulate a journey out. This may mean teaching them to read or tutoring for GED. It may mean counseling or tutoring for their children. It may mean getting medical attention. It may mean helping them fill out forms for job training or assistance and standing with them in the process. It may mean education on financial management which includes financial counseling and readjusting their family budget to focus more on needs than wants. It often means us paying rent or utilities and buying groceries for a season. It may take six months, a year or more.

It is personal, not trying to fit people into a box that may not be best for them but designed specifically for each unique situation. It opens people's eyes to the fact that poverty is less of a financial situation and more of a state of mind with traps that can be overcome. It knows when to release them and allow them to pursue the remainder of the journey with the empowerment they have received, with no strings attached.

It works. It works because it is done with dignity and discretion. It is accomplished in a genuine relationship, with accountability and a heavy dose of love. It leans heavily and completely on the One who loves them most and designed a destiny for them greater than they can imagine and that they can discover in faith and right choices.

It's contagious. Neighbors, friends and family begin to see this person or family doing well, making right choices and becoming free from the things that oppressed them. Their financial situation has improved. There is more joy in their home. It becomes an example and testimony to those around them.

Not only have we seen many stand on their feet and succeed, but of all the people we have helped, only one did not pay us back in full for the investment we made. We never asked for this. It wasn't even inferred. It came from sincere hearts filled with gratitude and wanting to invest in the next person who needed help.

I will never forget one woman. When she came to us, her home was in disarray, her children had behavior problems and were struggling in school. She was illiterate. We began to counsel her, tutor her children and teach her to read. A few months later, she came to me after Sunday worship and said, "Pastor Tom, will you be here a while?" I guess she was still new enough that she didn't know that Sundays for us meant arriving about 9 am and departing somewhere around 4 or 5 pm, depending on how many people wanted to talk after church. "Please wait here. I need to go home and get something," she said.

She came back about 20 minutes later. She was holding a plastic bag with something very heavy in it. She handed it to me. I could tell it was a large plastic jug full of coins.

She explained, "I always thought I was poor. You have taught me that I am not poor. I am rich in so many ways! Please take this. It's our spare money for when the food stamps run out. Give it to somebody who needs it more than me."

I brought our staff downstairs and poured the coins on our conference room table. I told them the story. Then we counted the coins. $32.23.

It was worth 1,000 times more than that. It was a sacrificial gift from a grateful heart. It remained a symbol to us of sacrifice and dignity coming into a changed life. We used it to help another family in need.

Do we really want to change lives? If the answer is yes, then there are some things to consider:

- Stop imposing your agenda. Listen to the people who are there. Learn from them. Seek to hear and understand their story. Invite them to tell you what they think the greatest needs are, then seek to serve them in that light.

A prominent national ministry came to Detroit some years ago to hold a conference at a major venue aimed at healing the city's wounds. The leaders met with some Detroit pastors to share their view of the source of the problems in the city and how to deal with them. At the end of their presentation, the pastor of a Detroit church stood and said, "You offend us. You come here from outside with your explanations of the problems in our city. Have you once asked what we see? Have you any consideration for our opinions and our role in this city? We are the ones who have worked in this city for decades. It's our children who have bled and died on these streets ..."

His poignant words need to be remembered by anyone who desires to help in the city.

- Seek every way to serve the people who are there making a difference. Offer ideas when invited to do so, but only when laced with prayer and after spending ample time learning and understanding from the people who have been serving in the city.

- Research what is happening in that community. There is no need to replicate what is already taking place. Instead, serve what is there and help it reach its potential.
- Understand that building relationships of trust takes time. Be patient and consistent.
- Don't begin if you don't plan to finish. There are too many fly-by-night efforts in the city.
- Don't look at people as a charity project. Look at them as a unique and special creation of God with a divine destiny waiting to be fulfilled.

Hear what two of our youth in the Bronx once said:

"No one wants to be looked at as a charity case or someone's personal project. Especially kids in the inner cities. Too many people come for that. To do something for charity. To build up a name for themselves. Personally, I don't want anyone's "charity." I don't feel I owe anything to someone who just wants to make a scene out of my very real life. Are you here to really help, or to be able to say you did something for this horrible place? Is it about you, or about us? Or rather, is it about God? We can tell when someone is for real, and when someone is just in it for themselves."

"Far too often, people come to the South Bronx to help these "poor people." When they leave, nothing has changed except the hearts of the people. They grow colder because of those that "help" in vain. If you wanna do something different, try doing it with love."

- Pray for them. Yes, prayer really does change things. The first thing it changes is your heart. The more you pray for those with whom you are hearing their stories and building relationships, God will give you His heart for them. He will also give you His plans. The greatest successes we have had in over 25 years of ministry in the city have not been the ideas we borrowed;

they came through prayer and desperation for healing through Christ's hands.

A South Bronx youth said, *"The best thing you can do for anyone you love is pray for them. If you don't pray for them, everything else you do is meaningless because you don't know God's heart for them."*

- Speak the truth. Once you have the relationship of trust, don't hold back from speaking the truth. Speak it with love and in a heart-language that they can understand, with relevance in their real world.
- Find ways to truly empower the people. Remember, band aids arealways short-term fixes. If a person, God forbid, has cancer, you don't put a band aid over the area where the disease is and hope it will cure what's on the inside. We need to get to the core of the issues. That takes thought, prayer, research, networking, strategizing, listening, and engaging in methods that produce long-term change.

Over the years, we have learned that the best methods to produce long-term change are never quick fixes. They take time to implement, to set into the hearts of people, and to produce the desired results. When the fruit of the labor begins to reveal itself, it lasts.

- Love them with genuine love. It doesn't matter what you look like and how different you are. People who are street smart know authenticity, and they know the opposite. Love them with 1 Corinthians 13 unconditional love.

Words from a South Bronx youth about love:

"When I first came to church, honestly, if God didn't open my eyes literally to see that the leader loved me with a different love (God's unconditional love that He placed in her heart for me) that I have never encountered, I would have never opened up to her. I was beyond guarded and didn't believe or trust anyone when they said they loved me. God literally opened my eyes for His purpose and to make me understand that she loved me differently; and with that being the foundation of our relationship – God's love, not hers – I wanted her, not

just allowed her, but wanted her to be involved in my life. I felt safe to open up to her because I knew deep inside that her love wasn't fake."

Many years ago, I received a call from a pastor from a small town in Western North Carolina. I really thought I was talking to one of Barney Fife's relatives from *The Andy Griffith Show.* He was country to the core. He shared with me that he had a burden for New York City and that he and his wife 'Nita (Anita) wanted to come and learn from us. Based on the recommendation of a pastor friend, we worked out a time for him to come.

Shane was fascinated about everything in the city. Driving down the street, we saw some children playing and cooling themselves off from an opened fire hydrant. Shane yelled, "Stop! Stop! I ain't never seen nothin' like this 'cept on TV! I gotta take a picture of this so I can show my kids I saw this in person!"

Talk about a fish out of water. There was no way this guy fit in. Which was why I panicked when he and his wife showed up at *The Harvest Center* in bright orange t-shirts and said, "Pastor Tom, what time does your kids program start? Me and 'Nita, we gonna go to the park and round you up some kids!" I just shook my head and prayed for God's mercy as they walked out the door.

About 20 minutes later, Shane called me. "Pastor Tom, what time did you say your kids program starts? I done got me about 20 kids and I'm gonna round up some more!"

Shortly after that, Shane and Anita walked in the door with 30 kids hanging all over them. His genuine heart had made a connection with these kids!

After the kids got settled into their seats for our children's program, Shane said, "Me and 'Nita, we gonna go for a walk!" I literally pled with God to keep them safe. A couple hours later, Shane came back and told us an emotional story.

He and Anita walked down Brook Avenue to 138th Street. They turned left and saw some gang bangers and drug dealers hanging out in front of a barber shop. Shane looked at his wife and said, "Hey 'Nita, watch this! I'm gonna do somethin' crazy!"

He walked over to one of the guys, got close to his shoulder and said, "Hey man, you look hard!"

That's not the introduction we advise in that context. But the love in Shane's heart was so large and so genuine that he won the favor of the guys there. Shane took a picture with them. Shane is standing in the middle of about 9 or 10 young men. He is wearing all their "bling" (necklaces and rings). His Yankees hat is on backwards, and everyone is smiling ear to ear.

After the picture, the owner of the barber shop approached Shane and said, "Can I give you a free haircut?" Shane responded, "Well, I don't need a haircut, but I'll let you give me a haircut if you let me tell y'all about Jesus!" Shane sat in the chair with all the young men around him and told them about Jesus' love for them with tears running down his face while he received a free haircut.

We know that seed will not return empty.

The way we tend to think, the very opposite should have happened. Someone that different and foreign to our community should not have had that kind of connection. That is probably true, but this package, though different on the outside, was filled with the powerful, compelling love of God. With God's authentic love, every bridge can be built, and every divide crossed to create a genuine connection with people, and with God.

If we want to make a difference in the lives of the suffering, the first step is to allow God's love to make a difference in us. Then that love can flow through us and help us to point people to the balm of healing only found in Jesus Christ and empower them toward the beautiful future God has designed for them, a future that will change their lives and change the lives of others through them.

Chapter Eleven

A Vision Reborn

"Behold, I will do something new..."

Isaiah 43:19 (NASB)

I would have never dreamed that God would use a hockey puck to send us on the next part of our journey.

Justin walked into my office with some questions about his student mission team visiting us from Metro Detroit. Just as he was about to ask his question, he saw a Detroit Red Wings hockey puck on my desk and said, "You're a Detroit Red Wings fan?!" I grew up in Detroit and yes, with exception of our legendary South Bronx team the Yankees, I'm a Detroit sports fan, especially hockey.

Justin and I began to talk about Detroit. He shared the needs in this great American city. I had not been back in many years, long before my daughter was born. He invited me to speak for his student ministry and to see what had happened in my hometown. He even promised tickets to a Red Wings game. How could I not accept!

I made plans to travel to Detroit in March 2004 to speak for Justin's student ministry and to take a needed week vacation. Many people questioned taking a week vacation in Detroit in the winter, but that was what we did.

I spoke for Justin's student ministry and we enjoyed our Red Wings game at the legendary Joe Louis Arena. We connected with old friends. We spent time driving around the city. That was where my heart began to break.

I have walked the streets of many devastated inner-city communities, but I was not prepared to see what I saw when I went back to my hometown of Detroit in 2004. They called the South Bronx "Vietnam" when we went there. When hurricane Katrina hit New Orleans, Detroiters said the economic "Katrina" hit them years before and it hadn't gone away.

This great city where I grew up was not at all the vibrant place I remembered. Woodward Avenue, the Broadway of Detroit and first paved road in America, was lined with empty stores and abandoned buildings. Communities were filled with abandoned homes. Office buildings were empty. More than half of the population had fled the city, leaving a crisis of infrastructure.

The Detroit city we visited in 2004 was the poorest major city in America. Over 45 percent of the population lived below the poverty line. Fifty percent of those lived below *half* of the poverty line. Unemployment in some communities was over 22 percent. The average combined annual household income in parts of East Detroit was $8,413, about $3,000 less than the South Bronx ten years before. Less than 22 percent of students graduated high school. Detroit had the highest foreclosure rate in the nation and was the most violent city in the nation nine out of 11 years.

And the most appalling statistic of all: there were more churches per capita in Detroit than any other city in the United States.

Something was desperately wrong.

I could not shake what I saw in Detroit. It was the epitome of urban neglect and decay. This city that I loved was in ruins and my God would not let me forget it. I prayed for Detroit every day for one year after that visit. Then God told me to go back, so I did.

I traveled to Detroit with two young men from the Bronx, Raul and Cephas, in March 2005. I did not fully understand the purpose of the trip; I just knew God wanted me to go.

We spent six days in Detroit. We walked the streets. We talked with people, asking them to tell us about their city. We spoke with people at bus stops and with students in front of high schools. We knocked on the doors of churches and met with pastors and leaders, not to share our story but to hear theirs.

We found in Detroit what we found in New York City when we began working there years before – churches that were not engaged in their community. Some pastors wanted to make a difference, but their community outreach was non-existent. To further complicate matters, we found that Detroit was one of the most racially divided cities in the nation. The infamous 8 Mile Road was a very real dividing line of people. We heard repeatedly from both sides that "people will not cross 8 Mile to help Detroit."

We also found churches with no interest in touching their own community. As the two young men and I met with one pastor, I asked him about community outreach. He responded, "We knocked on doors once inviting people to church. Nobody came so we're not going to do it again." I asked why God brought him to this location. He said, "We didn't come for the community; we came for the building … I have a radio show. Have you heard me?" It wasn't that he didn't know how to reach the needs around him; his heart was callous, and he truly didn't care. As we left his office, Raul wiped the dust off the bottom of his shoes.

Our time in Detroit in March 2005 opened our eyes to the reality of the needs in this city. But what did God want me to do about it?

I was invited to speak to the leadership of our denomination at their international headquarters that April by Dr. Raymond Culpepper, a cherished friend and prayer partner. He said, "Tom, I want you to share your theology. You can share stories, but I want you to focus on sharing your theology and approach to city reaching."

I had never really written down our theology, so I began doing so. It flowed quite easily and was an enjoyable experience, placing into words what God had taught us over the past 12 years and what our vision was for urban ministry.

I finished my presentation, printed it and laid it on my desk. I began to look for a document I needed in my files. As I did, I found a hanging file with no label on it. I am an organized person so that was rare. I pulled out the hanging file and opened the unmarked file folder inside. It was the paper I did on urban ministry in seminary in 1993 called *The Urban Harvest.* It consisted of an approach to reaching urban communities that included:

- Developing partnerships between suburban and urban Christians, organizations and churches.
- Establishing prayer initiatives uniting followers of Christ in prayer.
- Equipping existing and emerging leaders to implement strategies to reach the urban unchurched with the Gospel.
- Leading in relevant, strategic outreach that brings hope in a heart-language the people can understand.
- Empowering a local leadership team for ownership and sustainability of vision.

I laid the paper on my desk and began to look through it. As I did, I noticed something fascinating: the presentation I had just completed and *The Urban Harvest* paper I had written 12 years before were the same! Twelve years had passed, and the vision had not changed. It was still burning within me. I knew what God was saying: *Take this vision to Detroit and fulfill it there.*

Although the vision had not changed, the carrier of the vision had. We had been immersed in the urban community for 12 years, making that community our home and its people our family. We loved them, served them, cried with them, and sacrificed for them. We endured many hardships and much opposition. Our financial situation was difficult. My life had been threatened four times. Through all these things, we held on to the vision of lives being changed. We were passionate about God's hope replacing the despair and light permeating the darkness in our community. All that we endured changed me, making me more dependent on Him and much less on myself or anything else. It also gave me a deeper understanding of these communities and what it would take to bring change.

We went back to Detroit in June 2005, conducting two meetings with pastors where I shared the vision of reaching communities in Detroit and the story of what God had accomplished in the South Bronx. We only knew a handful of Metro Detroit pastors at that time, but they came and brought colleagues with them. The desire to make a difference was already there in their hearts, along with desperation for change to the current situation and trust to follow our leadership, a trust that humbled us as we moved forward. We planned an outreach for July partnering a church in the city and one from the suburbs. I would bring our leaders and workers from the Bronx to help launch the work.

July came. We went to an area of Southwest Detroit where poverty and neglect had taken a toll. After walking the streets, members of our team told me they were thankful they were raised in the projects in the South Bronx and Harlem and not in Detroit. It really was that bad.

When we began working in this community, we didn't know that we were on the dividing line of two gangs. We worked both territories and planned a block party in a large field on what happened to be that dividing line. The rival gang territories did not prevent people from both sides responding and working with us.

As we were walking the streets in different teams, one of my leaders came running. "Pastor Tom, we found these apartments. You have to see this." I hurried over and found two apartment buildings that were truly the worst I had seen - run down, decayed, and a center for drugs and prostitution. So much going on in this small complex, and it was completely absent of hope. We prayed and proceeded to the apartments.

What a spectacle we must have been, a group of Hispanic, Black and White strangers walking into their community singing with joy on our faces! The children took to our team quickly. Young men cautiously watched to see what was going on. Our ladies began conversations with moms, grandmothers and aunts and our youth with young teens who were there. After a short time, I asked everyone to come together in the courtyard. We did a couple humorous drama skits and then shared from our hearts about the love of Father God and the beautiful destiny He uniquely planned for each of them.

There was a lady who caught my eye. We could see on her face that the message of hope in Christ was impacting her heart. She began to cry and ran back into her apartment. I asked a mother there with her children, "What is that lady's name?" She said it was Pam.

I walked up the steps to Pam's door and began calling her through the screen door, "Hello Pam! I'm Pastor Tom." There was no answer.

"Pam, why don't you come back down here?" Still no answer. So, I called again, "Pam, come back out!"

"I can't!" she yelled from her second floor.

"Why not?" I asked.

"Because ya'll makin' me cry!"

"That's not us making you cry. That's the Spirit of God calling you by name! God loves you, Pam, and He wants to give you hope today!"

Pam came back outside, her face stained with tears. She was among many who made the first step on a new road to life and peace.

We returned each day that week, spending most of our time encouraging the people, listening to their stories, sharing with them about their God-designed destinies and about His love for them, and challenging them toward a new life of hope and peace. We learned that Pam was the mother figure to the gang members and dealers in the community. She was like the "Maria" that we had in the

Bronx, a mother figure and voice of authority for this community in Southwest Detroit.

We also got to know the gang members. They saw our hearts and the genuineness of our love for their people. They heard our stories from the Bronx and about our belief in the destinies God had designed for each of them. We bought a backboard and rim to replace the plywood and milk crate they were using to shoot basketball. They helped us install it. After three days, while standing in a circle with the gang leader and his gang and sharing about eternal destiny, Anthony, the gang leader, pointed to me, looked at his boys and said, "I'm out. I want what he's got." His gang members followed his lead to change their lives.

While all these wonderful things were happening, we noticed that the people from the local church were not responding. They stood with skepticism as we reached out to these poorest of the poor. Each day, less of them came to do outreach with us. At the end of the week, we took 19 people from these apartments to the church just four blocks away. They walked forward to join the church and become part of the fellowship. The church members looked at them from head to toe with criticism and disgust, obviously displeased with the way they were dressed. The people had worn their best jeans and T-shirts, but it wasn't good enough for this church. I had flashbacks to the legalism of the churches during our early years in the South Bronx.

Some of our team members overheard the church members calling these precious people "project rats." It was color-on-same-color racism. Someone said, "They forgot the pit from which they were dug." It was true. They forgot that their families once lived in communities just like this.

Pam moved to a house a few blocks away from the apartments. Her backyard joined the backyard of the church. In an entire year, neither the pastor nor anyone from the church visited her. Those that joined the church quit in just a few weeks. I didn't blame them.

But we didn't quit on them. We kept going back. Every trip to Detroit (which was about every six weeks at that time) involved spending an afternoon or evening with the people in this community. We would show up in the apartments or at Pam's house and the word would spread, "Pastor Tom is here!" The house would fill with people desperately hungry for the hope and unconditional love they felt when we were with them.

This was an area as bad as any I had worked in. The level of poverty and neglect was so high I couldn't imagine it being worse anywhere else in America. But the people? The people were beautiful, kind, loving, hungry for every word of hope coming out of our mouths.

"Pastor Tom" became the password. Sometimes I would knock on a door and receive no answer until I said, "It's Pastor Tom!" Late one night after a hockey game, I was near the community and wanted to follow up with a young father that lived there. John, a missionary to Lebanon, was with me. When we arrived at the community, John said he would stay in his car. I began to walk into the courtyard of the apartments. Then I heard footsteps running up behind me. It was John. "I thought you were going to stay in your car?" I asked. John said, "They can have my car. I'm worried about myself!"

As we walked into the courtyard, people began closing their curtains and turning off their lights. Two white men not from the community walking through the courtyard near 11:00 p.m. made people afraid something was about to happen, and not something good. It was an eerie feeling, but I continued.

I knocked on DeShawn's door. There was no answer, but I could hear the TV. I knocked again. Still no answer. I knocked a third time and I said loudly, "DeShawn, it's Pastor Tom!"

When I said that, lights in the apartments came back on, doors opened, and people came outside. Anthony, the former gang leader, came out of his apartment laughing. "I told ya'll! Ain't no cop gonna come in here at this time of night! It had to be Pastor Tom!"

We continued our visits to Detroit every six weeks, growing the network, imparting vision of reaching communities and pastoring the streets, empowering leaders and leading in outreach. With each visit, we would spend time in what became our favorite community in Detroit, visiting Pam's house and the apartments, loving the people.

Then one night a life-changing event happened. It was January 2007, about 9:00 p.m. Lidia and two staff from the Bronx – Karen and Raul - were with me. We had finished a day of meetings and were near the community. I had not heard from Anthony and I wanted to see him. We went to the apartments, greeted people, and I asked for Anthony. "He's in that house over there," pointing two blocks up the street.

I knew that house. I drove over, left Lidia and Karen in the car, and proceeded to the front door with Raul. The steps were broken and difficult to ascend. I knocked on the door. No answer. I knocked again. Still no answer. Then I said, "It's Pastor Tom from the Bronx!" The lights came on, the door opened, and we were invited in.

I spent about 30 minutes with Carman, the owner of that house, and his friend. Carman was leaning forward at the table listening intently to my words. Tears ran down his cheeks onto the table. Eventually, he reached out his hand, placed it on my arm, looked into my eyes and said, "How much longer will you be here, Pastor Tom?"

"Only a couple more days," I replied.

"Would you please knock on my neighbors' doors? They need hope, too!"

I was broken by his words. I restrained my emotions and prayed for Carman and his friend. We embraced and I returned to the car. As I sat down beside Lidia, tears filled my eyes. Here I was, four blocks from one church and six blocks from another in a community with people God loved so very much. Two churches were located so close, but their people were so calloused, prideful and stuck in their religious ways that a man had to ask someone from the Bronx to knock on his Detroit neighbors' doors because "They need hope, too!"

I looked at Lidia and quoted the words of Jesus when He was frustrated with His disciples who did not see the harvest before them in Samaria: *"You say the harvest is not yet, but I say look around you! The fields are ripe now and ready for harvest!"* (John 3:30).

Hope for the City was born on that night.

God did as He had done before in our lives: He gave a plan that made no human sense and sounded more like Joshua at Jericho than anything else. Part one: Call Christians in Detroit to the parking lot in front of Comerica Park (the Detroit Tigers baseball stadium) to worship the only One who is holy and pray to the only One who can help this city. Part two: Prayerwalk the streets of Downtown Detroit, saturating the heart of the city with prayer. Set up Prayer Stations to pray for the felt needs of people. Part three: Pray door-to-door for people in suffering communities. Bring hope to the doorsteps of people in a heart-language they can understand.

A prayer meeting in front of Comerica Park seemed to be a total impossibility for a small ministry with about a dozen churches in our network. It was like a Gideon commission. The request was made, nonetheless. With the son of a famous Detroit Tigers baseball player who loved God and our ministry, we approached Olympia Entertainment and asked for permission to hold a prayer and worship rally on the large parking lot in front of their baseball stadium and directly across from their offices and the Fox Theater. Not only were we given permission to use the parking lot, but the $20,000 fee was waived.

We sent out the word as best we could. I invited the pastors in our network to lead in prayer. We invited worship teams to join us. The choir from a large church in Detroit called me, hearing about the *Hope Rally,* and offered to come. A Gospel recording group and a Christian rap group also called. I informed each one that we would not be introducing people by name nor promoting ministries at this rally. The only names to be mentioned that day were that of God and His Son, Jesus. They all agreed to come, desiring to exalt His name more than their own.

As the day arrived, so did the clouds and the rain. It was an uncharacteristically cold day in July. We set up the stage and sound. People began to arrive, but the rain did not stop. I sat in my car praying, reminding the Lord of what He already knew: we had planned much for this event. We didn't want the rain to dampen it.

The parking lot was filling with people. I gave the word to begin the worship. As the worship began, the rain stopped.

Brothers and sisters in Christ, pastors and leaders in the city, came to the stage to lead in prayer. Worship continued in between those prayers. We prayed for children, for youth, for mothers and fathers. We prayed for schools and businesses. We prayed for churches and ministries. We prayed for forgiveness and for justice. We repented for our sins that have contributed to the ills of our city, especially the sin of indifference.

Then it was my turn to lead in prayer. I prayed as I was moved in my spirit to pray. I prayed against corruption in the highest places. I asked God to reveal the sources of corruption and bring them down. I asked God to raise up the fear of the Lord in the city and in seats of authority. With hearts united, we asked God to cleanse the city of the evil that had made its home there.

As I began to pray, a hole opened in the clouds above the parking lot. A ray of sunlight shone down upon us through the hole in the clouds. I felt the warmth on my back as I was praying. Some of the people took pictures of it. It was quite a sight.

I had frequently described what God did in the South Bronx in this way: God looked down and saw a small remnant of His people obediently praying over the community as He had directed us. He poked a hole in the cloud of oppression over our community and shined His favor down upon us. Change came in profound ways. We learned a vital lesson: His favor and His presence are what change things.

Now in Detroit, God was ready to do the same.

An executive assistant to the mayor of Detroit was with us at the *Hope Rally* that day. He and I became quite close friends, and Lidia with his wife. Just a couple months after our prayer and worship rally, corruption in the highest levels of city government was exposed. A scandal developed. In a meeting in the mayor's office, city officials tried to reason about what had happened and what do to next. My friend, the assistant to the mayor, stood up in the meeting and boldly shared his heart:

"Let me tell you why this crisis has happened. It has happened because a few months ago, godly people gathered down Woodward Avenue in front of Comerica Park and prayed for our city. They prayed for injustice to cease and corruption to be exposed. They prayed for God to cleanse our city. God is answering their prayers!"

People thought he would be fired. When leaders in the Mayor's office met to discuss who to dismiss, the mayor walked in and said, "You can fire whoever you want except for Phillip (our friend). He keeps his job." Why would the mayor say that? I believe the mayor knew that what Phillip said was true. Phillip served that mayor until that mayor was removed from office. He served the next two mayors as well.

Our vision for reaching the city, for bringing hope door-to-door and conducting relevant outreach in the communities that needed it most, was shared and accepted at the *Hope Rally*. Shortly after, we conducted our first Downtown Prayerwalk. We saturated the streets of the heart of the city with prayer. Dozens of people came. We broke into five prayer teams. Each prayer team had appointed leaders and a map of the area they were to prayerwalk. The map noted strategic places to stop and pray: at the courthouse, businesses, banks, schools and universities, and government offices. We prayed at the GM Headquarters for all the families who lost jobs and for new jobs to come into the area. At a university, we prayed for college students and professors. At the Blue Cross Blue Shield building, we prayed for those who were sick without insurance and for fairness and compassion in that industry. We prayed at historical sites, like Campus Martius and Grand Circus Park.

We prayed in front of boarded up buildings where businesses once stood and pleaded with God for businesses to return to Detroit. The reality of the crisis in Detroit was noticeably clear before our eyes as store after store was boarded up and building after building abandoned.

At churches, we prayed for revival that would not stir emotions but that would bring change, a revival that would stir the church to become the agent of change in the community around it. We prayed for God to bring a cleansing from the pulpit to the pew to the altar. As my group was praying at a prominent downtown church, a thunderstorm came. We stood under the canopy praying there for nearly half an hour. Two other pastors were with me. Each one began to pray for the true fire of God to fall bringing conviction, renewal and cleansing to the church.

All the prayer teams concluded the prayerwalk at City Hall, by *The Spirit of Detroit* statue and the seal of Detroit, where we joined together in a final corporate prayer. I was interrupted three times during my final remarks as fire trucks sped by us with their sirens blasting. Finally, we were able to conclude the prayerwalk with corporate prayer.

Later that evening, I received a call from one of the pastors who was praying with me under the church canopy during the thunderstorm. The pastor said, "Do you remember what we prayed at that church during the rainstorm? Do you remember praying for the fire of God to fall? Do you remember the fire trucks that went by when we met for the final prayer? Did you hear what happened? A three-alarm fire broke out in a church downtown!" I don't think that our prayers had anything to do with that fire, but I tell you that

I shook a little bit in my shoes when that pastor called me that night. I believed God heard our prayers for the city.

The Spirit of Detroit at City Hall is probably the city's most defining site. It is a sculpture of a man holding a sphere in one hand and a family in the other. The sphere emanating rays in the left hand represents God. The family in the right hand – father, mother and child – have their hands raised in worship. The sculptor states that this represents the center of human relationships. On the wall behind the sculpture are written words that the sculptor says are meant to be the focus of it all:

"Now the Lord is the Spirit: and where the Spirit of the Lord is, there is liberty" (2 Corinthians 3:17 NASB).

The Spirit of Detroit sculpture has the words *"Now the Lord is that Spirit . . ."*

On the wall adjacent to this beautiful sculpture is the Seal of Detroit. It depicts a woman crying with a city burning behind her. A second woman is consoling her with a rebuilt city behind her. In 1805, the city of Detroit burned to the ground. Only a few stone structures remained. It took years to rebuild the city. When they did, they declared Campus Martius the city center and they adopted the motto of the city *Speramus meliora. Resurgit cineribus.* These Latin words written on the Seal mean *"We hope for better things. It will rise from the ashes."*

These words reminded me of the words so special to us from Isaiah 61: God will bring *beauty from ashes.* In this city of hopelessness, God called us to be a part of bringing beauty from ashes and hope in place of despair.

As people began to walk and pray over their city, their hearts were broken. They began to see the city as God sees it. Their disdain for their city was replaced with compassion and brokenness, and the understanding that things could really change if God's people united in prayer and outreach.

And so, we did.

The *Hope for the City* network began to grow. We established prayer stations in strategic areas in Downtown Detroit, focusing on City Hall and Campus Martius. Lines of people would form, waiting for prayer. Sometimes cars and even city buses would stop, asking for prayer. Once a man got off a bus two blocks away. He came to our prayer station on the sidewalk at City Hall and said, "I felt something strong! I felt hope! I started walking in this direction until I saw you!" At the same location a year later, a lady came to us and said, "I know you don't remember me, but last year I was homeless and without a job. My father was also. I came by your prayer station and you prayed for me. You see that building?" she said as she pointed to a nearby office building. "My office is on the sixth floor. I have a home now, and my father also has a job now. *I know it's because you prayed!"*

On another occasion, a young lady came by the prayer station with her small child. She was about to be evicted from her home and she had no place to go. Lidia took considerable time to talk with her and encourage her to have faith in God who loves her and would take care of her. After about 30 minutes, while Lidia was still sharing with her and listening to her story, a man came to the same prayer station and asked, "What is this?" We explained our purpose and then asked him, "Do you work around here?" He said, "Yes, I work for the Red Cross. I specifically work to assist displaced single moms with housing options." We looked at each other beaming and said, "Can we introduce you to someone?" At that moment, the young mother's prayer was answered. A few years later, she came running to us at the same prayer station. "Do you remember me?" She shared about how she was thriving while her daughter grabbed prayer flyers and began giving them to passersby.

Divine appointments. Lives changed because we followed God's call to bring hope outside where the people were, to walk among the people as Jesus did. Our prayer stations have a banner that says,

"Hope offered here!" and "God cares!" Day after day, we realized that was the message people desperately needed to hear.

We were informed by a policeman that we needed to apply for a permit. We had never heard this before in any other location, but we obliged. I was given a 30-page application that movie directors complete when closing off streets to film a movie. I completed every question with the supporting documentation and then received this response from city hall: "You don't have to apply for an application. This is your constitutional right." We already knew that.

Another encounter with a police officer took place when a man began loudly mocking us and those stopping for prayer. The more we ignored him, the louder and more belligerent he became. I approached a police officer nearby and asked if he could assist us. Without saying a word to me, he went directly to the man, speaking sternly to him with his face only inches from the man's face. The man left, as did the officer, without giving me an opportunity to thank him. A few hours later, I saw that policeman walking down the block and I thanked him. He said, "What you are doing is so important here. Our city needs this. Please don't stop doing this!"

We prayed in communities more than we prayed at prayer stations. We would walk through the streets, going door-to-door, saying, "Hello sir. I'm Tom Grassano. I am helping the pastor down the street. I am not here to preach at you. I have no literature to give you. I am not here to invite you to church. I am here because God put it into our hearts to pray for every family on this block. How can I pray for you today?"

Residents cautioned us not to walk their streets. There was too much blood spilled there. Too many guns carried by too many angry, hurting people with no reason to live. The people in some communities told us that they were too afraid to walk their own streets. But something compelled us: *There are hurting people here and they need to know there is hope.* We continued walking the streets and loving people.

Over and over, people broke down and wept at their doors. Sometimes the prayer would be short. Sometimes we would stay for long periods of time getting to know the family and hear their story. Through this, we were able to encounter the needs of families and address them. We were able to connect them with a church that cared and that we were equipping to empower the people in their community.

Life change began to happen through those encounters. On one occasion in East Detroit, my daughter Angel met a lady named Cassandra at her door. Angel invited Cassandra and her children to the Community Family Day that would take place later that week and then offered to pray for Cassandra. One of Cassandra's biggest concerns was the financial condition of her family due to her loss of employment. As Angel prayed for God to show Cassandra how much He loved her, Cassandra began to cry. Angel spent quite a bit of time encouraging her and praying with her.

Cassandra came to the Community Family Day. She looked around until she found Angel and gave her the news, "I got a job!" God answered the prayer. Cassandra was in church with her children the next day.

A few years into the work in Detroit, a pastor from the suburbs accompanied me as we completed the logistics at a site where outreach would begin the next week. We had a final meeting over lunch that day with the *Hope for the City* leadership before launching the summer outreach intensive. On the way to that meeting, the pastor and I stopped by a church who wanted to learn more about *Hope for the City.*

This church leads a thriving homeless ministry downtown. While waiting for the staff member who wanted to meet with me, a homeless man I knew named Chris approached me. We embraced and began to talk. After a few minutes Chris said, "My counseling session will begin in a few minutes. I don't want to disrespect you, but I'll have to go when the counselor comes!"

I informed Chris that was no problem at all and that I was happy to see him. His counselor approached, saw me, jumped back a step and said, "Pastor Tom! What are you doing all the way over here from the South Bronx?"

I looked into his eyes trying to discern if I knew him. Then he said, "You remember me, don't you? I'm James Harris, the homeless alcoholic who used to come into your Bible study the first year you were on Brook Avenue in the South Bronx!"

I could not believe who was standing in front of me. It had been 16 or 17 years but yes, I remembered James, the filthy, smelly homeless man who would come into our Bible studies on Wednesday nights just to warm himself from the cold. He never seemed to listen to anything I would say and never seemed to care about any prayer I ever prayed over him.

James told me his story about how God took him from the South Bronx to Chicago and then to Detroit. God changed his life. He went back to school and became a certified counselor. Now he is helping people who were just like him. He stuck his finger in my chest and laughed as he said, "It's all your fault!"

The pastor with me wept. I remembered the words of Pastor Dave Wilkerson when we began our work, "You are establishing a spiritual hospital, a place where many will come, be healed, and go their ways. You will never know what happens to most of them until heaven." God allowed me to know what happened to James.

From that defining moment in the parking lot of Comerica Park, hundreds of lives have been changed. With the tools in hand that we had forged over the years in the Bronx, we pressed forward in Detroit uniting followers of Christ from many backgrounds in prayer and serving, empowering pastors and leaders, leading relevant outreach strategies, and walking streets neglected for years. Our diligence brought great results. We began to accomplish several things at once: reach lost and hurting souls, unite the church, cast vision and empower for city reaching, and stand boldly against the things that have thwarted the healing of this city. Outreach has taken place across the city bringing hope to people. Churches have united and changed from inward focus to vision and implemented strategies for their communities. As one pastor stated, "Urban Harvest Ministries changed the DNA of our church, but they changed it in me first!" We see the evidence of that with the impact of his church in their community.

Another pastor said, "You incarnate hope for this city." That is our mission.

One of the greatest blessings from *Hope for the City* has been the unity among those involved. Churches across a wide spectrum of denominations, race and geography have united in this effort. Different liturgy and expressions of faith have been respected and have never deterred from that which binds us together: vision for our city and belief that Christ is the answer. While each had fellowship in their own movements, they found a deep love and commitment to one another and to the mission. This has created some of the deepest, most meaningful, and most highly valued relationships I have ever had.

There are more stories of the amazing things God has done through this ministryin this city than I could ever fit into this chapter. It would take an entire book! But I must share one more story, one of the most memorable ones for me on the streets of Detroit.

A few years ago, as we turned down a street while prayerwalking in East Detroit, I saw a young man standing halfway down the block, smoking a "blunt" and impressing the girls with his dancing. Having walked the streets of the inner city for over 20 years, it has become easy to pick out the man in charge of drugs and gangs. I just didn't know how high up the ladder he would be.

Being *Hope for the City* week, we had outreach teams serving in many of the desperate and hurting communities of Detroit. On that night, there were more than four dozen people saturating the streets in prayer and relational outreach in this East Detroit community. I had six people in my group – my son, a Detroit pastor and his co-worker, a Russian pastor and son, and a member of the Russian congregation who spoke no English and interceded the entire time we walked the streets. We certainly stood out in this community.

I approached this young man and introduced myself, breaking the ice with my comments about his impressive dancing. The conversation comfortably moved from introductions to small talk to a message from 1 Corinthians 13 that spoke to their hearts:

"There is a love that will not fail you. It will not abuse you and leave you cold and hurting. There is a love that is unconditional. It is pure and kind. It doesn't keep a record of the things you have done wrong. It treats you with respect and hopes the best for you. It protects you and heals your wounds. It is the love that led Jesus to the cross ... for you."

Tears began to flow down the cheeks of some of the young ladies as God spoke tenderly to the wounds of their hearts compelling them to a greater love than they had ever known. The young men stood silent and still, captured by a Spirit so strong at that moment that we could feel it all around us. *Where two or three are gathered in His name, He is there* (Matthew 18:20). We knew without doubt that was true that night.

Jayden didn't want to relinquish the focus of attention, but the more I spoke, the more he gave me the right to speak. I finally looked at him and shared what God had placed in my heart. "You have too many wounds, young man. You lay awake at night in the darkness of your room thinking about the pain. It doesn't go away, and you wonder if it will ever end." His eyes and his silence spoke volumes of yearning to be free of the pain that his life and his choices had brought to him.

Then I spoke words that brought a much stronger reaction, as I knew they would. "I feel sorry for you, Jayden." He didn't like that comment. "I feel sorry for you because, if you don't accept the freedom and love that God has waiting for you, one day you will stand before Him and He will ask you, 'What did you do with the talent, personality and leadership that I gave you?' What will you say, Jayden?" I paused, and then said, "But you can begin a new life … right here, right now."

About that time, a carload of his crew pulled up, making rather colorfulremarks. I immediately said to all who were listening, "Don't let anyone steal from you what you know is true right now."

With the new group watching, I asked if they wanted to begin a new life at that very moment. From the heart, all of them said yes. We prayed.

Finishing our prayer, we opened our eyes and saw a miracle. Something had taken place in Jayden. The touch of God was so powerful on his life that it changed his countenance. Even his eyes, bloodshot from weed and who knows what else before we arrived, were now crystal clear, revealing a beautiful green color we could not see before. His demeanor had completely changed. Humility and peace had flooded into his heart as the very real and powerful love of God began to cleanse, heal, and infuse hope into his broken soul.

One of the ones who had driven up suddenly said, "Jayden, what happened to your face?" He saw the transformation. The Detroit pastor with us shared the same Truth with the ones who had just arrived. They opened their hearts to Christ's love, and their lives were changed, too.

I kept in touch with Jayden. A year later, he walked two and a half hours to our Community Family Day with his little daughter in a broken baby carriage because he didn't have car fare. I asked him why he did it. He said, "Are you kidding? I wouldn't miss this for anything!" God had begun a wonderful work in his life.

I saw Carman three years after that encounter in his home in January 2007. I was speaking on a Sunday morning in a church not terribly far from the community where I met him. I spotted him in the congregation while I was speaking. Well-dressed, with a smile on his face, he looked good.

He humbly walked up to me after church. "Do you remember me, Pastor Tom?"

"Of course, I do, Carman. I have prayed for you for the past three years." What a beautiful reunion that day.

And Anthony? Several years after that first outreach in Southwest Detroit, I received a phone call from a number I did not know. When I answered, I heard a familiar voice.

"Pastor Tom, it's Anthony from Spaulding Court. Do you remember me?" Of course, I did.

"I got locked up. They took my phone and I never got it back. But I just found your card with your number! I wanted to tell you that me and Tanya and the baby are doing good. We have jobs. We have a good apartment. God has been good to us. Thank you for all you did for us. We know what we have now is because of you."

No, not because of me.

Because of the One who sent me.

Chapter Twelve

Tell the Nations

"Go and make disciples of all the nations."

Matthew 28:19

As long as I can remember, I have had an interest in the nations. When I was young, I would study world maps and read about other countries. I studied ethnomusicology during my undergraduate and graduate degrees in music, at times working folk rhythms from various cultures into my compositions. My father traveled to 70 nations in ministry. From his stories and the stories of many missionaries who stayed in our home and ate at our table, I grew up surrounded by God's heart for the nations. Then, I married a missionary's daughter. God surrounded me with His love for the world.

I made two international trips with my parents as a teenager, one to Mexico and another to Puerto Rico. Both of those trips made an impact on my young life, but it was when I spent several weeks serving in Mexico the summer of my sophomore year in college that the trajectory of my life began to change. I went there to teach in a summer music camp and to work with youth. I enjoyed working with the people and the youth much more than teaching music. God began to stir something in my life. I wanted to serve people. I felt compassion for the suffering in the world and a passion for the eternal hope in the Gospel.

By the time we moved to the Bronx, I had traveled to 18 nations, empowering leaders and leading in outreach. Seeing the Acts of the Apostles still being written in the countries I visited was more than compelling; it was life changing. Miracles and healings were taking place just like in the Bible. In some countries, entire towns and villages were being impacted by the Gospel message. It was as if they were living Acts 17:6 where the followers of Christ were described as those who were turning the world upside down. This was, and still is, normal in many places around the world. It made me yearn for it in my own nation. It also made me hunger to be around it.

I have traveled to 24 nations in Latin America, the Caribbean, Europe and Asia thus far in my life. I have walked the streets of slums in large cities and the dirt roads of remote villages among indigenous people. I have watched children foraging for food in garbage dumps and I have brought food and vitamins to villages with high infant mortality rates. I have served where the Gospel is accepted and where people worship freely. I have also served where there is great suffering and persecution for those who follow Jesus.

I have found stark differences between faith in my nation and faith in many places around the world. Where self-promotion, self-preservation, and self-reliance are typical in America, self-denial, sacrifice, and complete dependence on God are commonplace in the church in the two-thirds world. Where we promote a gospel of prosperity, they preach a gospel for the poor. Where we are attendees and hearers of the Word, they are disciple-making disciples who multiply their faith. We fear man; they fear God. We believe in relative truth. They believe in absolute truth, and God proves Himself to them every day. While we look for the greatest conveniences for our lifestyles and our faith, in many, many places there is a significant cost to serving Jesus and a great joy among those who do.

No wonder the God of scripture proves to them every day that *"Jesus Christ is the same yesterday, today and forever"* (Hebrews

13:8). He does the same things for them that He did for the New Testament Christians and for anyone who calls on Him in faith.

My wife spent her teenage years in Guatemala during the Civil War that broughtso much suffering and pain to the country. She was also there for the 1976 earthquake that killed 23,000, injured nearly 80,000, and left hundreds of thousands homeless and displaced. It was during those years that the people turned to God and a revival swept the nation. During the same time in neighboring El Salvador, 42 pastors in one denomination alone were killed by leftist guerillas. Despite these things, people's faith in and hunger for God spawned unceasing testimonies of divine protection, provision, and miracles. So many lives were being changed that, in some towns, the bars closed, and the jails were left empty.

The summer after completing my doctorate, my wife and I visited Chile and Argentina. We visited my wife's family in Chile, and I ministered in churches in Santiago, Valparaiso, and Concepcion. I do not remember what I spoke about in a church in Santiago one Sunday, but I do remember what God did after the message. The pastor led his congregation to observe the ordinance of communion. A member of the church who had been blind for 35 years was present. As he partook of the bread and the cup, the Lord opened his eyes. Thirty-five years of darkness disappeared in a moment. It did not happen with noise and fanfare. In a simple act of personal worship, Jesus touched the man's eyes, and he could see.

From Chile, we went to Argentina where I taught for a couple weeks at a seminary in Buenos Aires. I love that city, one of my favorites that I have visited. The commercial center is a bustling area of shops and restaurants with street musicians at every turn. I saw a wonderful opportunity to do outreach at this commercial center. I shared this with the seminary students and the seminary director. The students were excited. After a few days of preparation, we were ready to go.

We congregated at the intersection of two large pedestrian streets in the middle of the commercial center. Knowing that Argentinians love music and that there is a large presence of those with Italian heritage, I began by singing some arias from Italian operas. Half of the seminary students formed a semi-circle around me as the others stood around in the periphery. About 60 pedestrians stopped to listen. I sang a few arias and then sang an old Andrae Crouch song in Spanish, *The Blood (of Jesus) Will Never Lose Its Power.*

Some of the seminary students then shared powerful testimonies of where they had come from and how Jesus had changed their lives. The students began to pray with people in the crowd. I watched as a young man fell to his knees weeping. We learned his story after we finished the outreach.

This 19-year-old young man had lost hope and had given up on life. He had left a suicide note in his home and was on his way to end it all. As he was walking to the place he had chosen to kill himself, he prayed, "God, if You are real, and if You really care about me, this is Your last chance." By God's divine providence, he stumbled on our gathering a few minutes after that prayer.

He gave his life to Christ and found the hope he had been looking for. The darkness was lifted, and the love of God filled the emptiness of his soul. The students invited him to go back to the seminary with them where they spent hours talking, singing, sharing stories and encouraging their new friend. Somewhere around 2:00 a.m. the young man remembered that he had left a suicide note at home. He rushed home to tell his family about the new life that God had given him.

The boy was desperate. The message was true. The timing was prepared in heaven. God's people decided to get out of the church, out of the seminary walls, and bring hope to the streets of the city. Because of that, this young man's life was eternally changed.

I returned to Argentina several years later with a team of pastors and college students. Ministering in a church in Buenos Aires, a man came forward asking for prayer. He rolled up his sleeves to reveal some form of skin disease that he said covered his entire body. He wept as we prayed for him. The altar was filled with people asking for prayer. As we continued praying with others, the man came to us asking for prayer a second time. I felt great compassion for him. After we prayed for him and moved on to pray with others, the man moved to the side, lifted his hands and began to praise the Lord. Healing had not come, but he chose to praise the Lord anyway.

While praising the Lord with his hands raised in worship, the man opened his eyes and saw that the skin on his arms was completely healed. He began to look inside his shirt and realized God had healed him.

"Jesus Christ is the same yesterday, today and forever" (Hebrews 13:8).

Many years later, God gave an opportunity for our young adults in the Bronx to experience what we had experienced in other nations. A missionary to Mexico visited us in the Bronx in 1999. He observed our drama ministry and felt like God could use us in Cuba. We accepted his invitation. God miraculously provided the funds to go.

We could not enter Cuba directly from the U.S., nor could we enter as a ministry team. Going through Mexico, we entered as a drama troupe from New York City with their professor.

Our first trip to Cuba was the first and only mission trip overseas that I have made without an itinerary. We went to walk faithfully, to serve the people, and to pray God would open doors. He was ever so faithful to do just that.

We spent our first day getting to know our hosts who graciously opened their home to us even though that was not generally accepted in Communist Cuba. They were hospitable but also apprehensive about what we would do there and how we could potentially expose them to the Communist Party informant that lived down the street.

The house was adequate; the supplies in Cuba were not. There was water four to six hours a day in two-hour intervals. The people did not know exactly when that would be, so they kept large buckets under their faucets and spigots to catch the water for later use. Most often a bath was a bucket wash using a large ladle to wet oneself and then rinse after lathering up.

Five young men and I stayed in a small bedroom with three twin beds. It was hot. The only time to cool off was during a bucket wash or shower. Food was scarce. The government rations food and allows ridiculously small monthly allotments for each family – seven pounds of rice, one pound of beans, a bottle of cooking oil, and small quantities of coffee, sugar, chicken and eggs. Children get one liter of milk per month. This is true for all citizens of Cuba, unless they work for the government or military, in which case they have an abundance. The rest of the food was acquired mostly on the black market.

On our first full day, we split into two groups and went prayerwalking. An hour into the walk, one of my group came running up to me. "Pastor Tom, we found a youth block party! They want us to perform!" The block party was led by the Communist Youth Organization, and surely enough, they asked us to perform. We had developed dramas, mimes, human videos and rhythm routines with powerful messages. I explained to the leader that a lot of our drama presentations express our faith. He said, "It is good for cultural interchange." That was fine with me.

We had choreographed Gloria Estefan's song *Coming Out of the Dark* and were excited to perform it for the Cuban audience. We began our performance with that song. The leader of the Youth Organization informed me that her music was banned in Cuba because of her father's participation in the resistance. They understood that we were ignorant to that, and they laughed at our mistake. They enjoyed the remainder of our performance.

After our performance, the community Communist leader invited me into hishome where he served me coffee and refreshments. Our group interacted and played soccer with the Cuban youth. We spoke about many things. It was there that I learned that all of Cuba knew about the South Bronx. Fidel Castro used our community to show his nation the failure of capitalism and American democracy. God used the "spectacle" of where we came from to open doors for Him. The community leader was impressed with our performance and asked my permission to inform his colleagues about us so that we could perform in other places.

Our performance that day led to many open doors and invitations, so much so that the church leaders became a little nervous. Once they saw how God had ordained this and how He was using it, they invited us to their churches.

We were invited to a house church on a Friday night led by an older, humble pastor with many years of experience. It was an honor to be with him. When we arrived, we saw a few dozen people standing in the doorway and peering in windows to be able to listen to the service because the house had filled. The pastor approached me and said, "We need to move the meeting into the yard. There are many people. If we do not, they cannot hear." Knowing what he was saying and the risks involved, I said, "Pastor, whatever you desire is fine with us. We are here to serve you."

As we began to perform, many people from the community came. By God's providence, we began to perform when the evening television programming had finished. So many came that the yard and the three-way intersection in front of us filled with people. The driver of a city bus that could not pass through the crowd turned off his engine and allowed the passengers to hear our presentation.

As I was sharing the gospel, the Communist leader for that community arrived and approached the pastor. "What is going on here?" he asked. The pastor shared that a drama troupe visiting from the United States had performed for the people and that I was their leader. The man stayed for a few minutes, listening to my words. Then he looked at the pastor and said, "This is good for our community. Please continue," and he walked away.

Doors opened in the church and in the community. We were blessed by every opportunity. We were surprised when we received an invitation to perform for a community celebration for Fidel Castro's birthday in Havana. What an opportunity! I accepted immediately.

One of the dramas we performed was a 15-minute depiction of the fall of man and the redemption of Christ. I shared from the "text" (the Bible) that the story came from. I was concerned about some police down the block. Their eyes were very fixed on us until a city bus came and blocked their view for the remainder of the performance.

Many people fought to get my eye while I was sharing and gave a nod and a smile, acknowledging that they understood the message. Eternal seed was sown that day.

We visited church services in many areas, some in decent buildings and some in small, rustic ones that were in disrepair. We conducted a service in a community filled with witchcraft where a lady, who was one of the main witches in the community, had come to Christ. Her transformed life became a compelling witness to her neighbors.

In a Chevy and a Packard made in the late 1950's, we drove to a town about two and a half hours from Havana. It was a small village with a chicken farm. The government decided that the people in this village would not be rationed eggs because they could potentially steal eggs from the chicken farm and say they were part of their monthly ration. Thus, no eggs were allowed in this village.

We were the first Americans to visit this village since the revolution nearly 40 years before. All the villagers came to a community meeting house where we spent time with them and performed for them. They prepared rooms in their homes for us to stay and they cooked one of the most delicious meals I have ever eaten, though quite difficult to eat because of the sacrifices made to prepare it. One family slaughtered their only pig and another their only turkey to prepare that meal for us.

Early the next morning, one of the church leaders drove to adjacent villages to round up enough eggs so that we could have a bountiful breakfast. We felt so ashamed. Who are we that they would sacrifice so much for us? I spread the word with our team to eat one portion only and leave plenty of leftovers for the people. We left that village with a much greater blessing than we could have ever given them.

After returning to Havana, we visited another church. We performed drama, shared testimonies, and I shared an exhortation from the Word. After the service, as we were greeting people and conversing with them (most of my team spoke Spanish), the one team member with no Spanish language ability came to me with a pale, bewildered look on her face and an infant in her arms. She said, "I was admiring this lady's baby and then she put the baby in my arms and walked out the door!" The pastor ran out the door and found the woman walking down the street, crying. She had given her baby to our team member to bring back to the United States because, "I know he will have a much better life than I can give him here." We returned the child, expressed our love for the lady, prayed for her, and the pastor did the rest.

On our last day of this trip to Cuba, we were invited to perform in a folklore theater in Havana. The director of the theater ran up to me after the performance with tears in his eyes, grabbed me with both arms and said, "Today, you have made the Invisible visible to me!" He had probably never heard the words of Paul the Apostle in Colossians 1:15, but those words became reality to him that day: *"Christ is the visible image of the invisible God."*

As I look back over three decades of ministry, there has not been one time in every place I have been that I have not found someone by divine appointment to encourage and give this glorious message of hope. When we walk among the people as Jesus did, God opens the doors. He is waiting for us to bring His hope to those that He loves and died for.

One of the lessons I have learned through serving in the inner city and in many nations is this: the world doesn't need our "fluff and stuff." They need hope. They need to see the message of the cross lived out in the lives of believers with sincere and authentic faith. They need for us to show them God's unconditional love in relevant ways, with His truth on our lips, and His hope in our hearts.

"Let my heart be broken with the things that break the heart of God." This is the prayer Bob Pierce prayed and wrote in his Bible decades ago after visiting suffering children on the South Korean island of Koje-do. Through this prayer and his open heart, God guided him to establish the ministry of Samaritan's Purse that has touched people in need across the earth. Imagine what could be birthed to reach the hurting and hopeless around the world if all of us would pray that same prayer.

Chapter Thirteen

A Beauty that Pleases the Soul

"No eye has seen, no ear has heard, and no mind has even imagined what God has prepared for those who love Him."

1 Corinthians 2:9

Our heritage of faith is one of the most valuable gifts we have been given on earth. Much of what we have accomplished in our lives has taken place because of the trails that were blazed before us. Parents and grandparents who held nothing back in serving God made the path clear. Loving the Lord God with all our hearts, souls, minds and strength, and loving our neighbors as ourselves were the choices laid before us that would become the guiding lights of our lives.

My heritage of faith began with my grandparents, Benedetto Grassano and Camiglia Virelli. Camiglia Virelli was born to Italian immigrant parents in lower Manhattan on Front Street near the South Street Seaport. Her father, Vito, owned a butcher shop and a small restaurant. Camiglia grew up playing on the steps of the Federal Building on Wall Street and in Battery Park, with her brothers occasionally sneaking a swim in the Hudson with a view of the Statue of Liberty. Camiglia's family moved to Borough Park, Brooklyn, and Camiglia acquired a job making Hickey Freeman suits in the garment district of Manhattan.

Benedetto Grassano was born in Ferrandina, Italy, near the town of Grassano in the region of Basilicata. Benedetto means "blessed" in Italian. Interestingly, the name at the train station in Grassano, Italy is "Benedetto Grassano," which means Blessed Grassano.

The only son of nine children, his responsibilities were great in the home, helping his parents, Tomasso and Maria Ungaro Grassano, and his sisters. He was a shepherd, keeping his sheep in a little cave in the back of his humble home. He would graze his sheep among the olive trees that filled the hills outside of his hometown. Benedetto's peaceful life was interrupted with World War I. He served in that bitter war, seeing a cousin killed beside him. Afterwards, he returned to Ferrandina to resume the life of a shepherd.

Southern Italy was poor, ravaged with malaria and neglected by Rome after World War I. Peasants worked 364 days a year, taking only December 25 to enjoy the town celebration of Christmas and special meals with family and friends. Days were long and hard. Family was the most important treasure on earth.

Carlo Levi, a writer, doctor and painter turned political activist, was exiled to Grassano and Gagliano in Basilicata in 1935 by Mussolini. He loved the village of Grassano. He kept a diary during his exile later published into the book *Christ Stopped at Eboli.* "Christ did stop at Eboli," Levi said, "where the road and the railway leave the coast of Salerno ... Christ never came this far . . . No one has come to this land except as an enemy, a conqueror, or a visitor devoid of understanding. The seasons pass today over the toil of the peasants just as they did three thousand years before Christ; no message, human or divine, has reached this stubborn poverty.[1]" As a result, the people of Basilicata, like my grandfather and his family, put no hope in Rome. All their hope was in New York City.

Benedetto's eldest sister Frances married Leonardo Grieco who moved to New York City. Frances died after bearing her second child. As the custom dictated, Leonardo asked for the next available sister to become his bride and raise his children. In 1920, at 22 years old with hope and a destiny before him, Benedetto left home on a horse-drawn carriage with his sister Antoinetta and cousin Tommy Montefinese and boarded a ship in Naples for a two-week trip to New York City. Benedetto left all that he knew in Italy for a brand-new world with one suitcase, hope and a dream. Ironically, the ship upon which they traveled from Naples to New York City was called the "Providence."

After the trek through Ellis Island, Benedetto landed in Hoboken, New Jersey. He later moved to Brooklyn and acquired his first job working under Manhattan digging subway tunnels. He then laid concrete for the Tri-Boro Bridge. He met Camiglia at a celebration and dance for people from Ferrandina. They fell in love and were married. They were a typical Italian family. Benedetto made his own wine in their basement.

They lived in a home owned by Camiglia's father Vito, beside the Rectory which was adjacent to Holy Spirit Catholic Church. Camiglia's brother, Joey, was ailing with cancer. His prognosis was not good.

Giulia worked in the garment district in Manhattan with Camiglia. We don't know much about her but her name and her role in changing the history of an entire family with a few words. One day, Giulia approached Camiglia at work and said, "Do you know that Jesus loves you so much that He died just for you?"

Camiglia had never heard it this way before. Church for her was form and cultural tradition. It had little to do with everyday life. It was done more out of obligation than a passion for worship and knowing a loving God. But underneath the form and tradition was a woman who was thirsty, like the woman Jesus met at the well in John chapter 4, for spiritual water that would truly satisfy, and for a faith that was alive and would satisfy her soul.

Giulia invited Camiglia to a little store front Italian church in Downtown Brooklyn. She went with her brother, Joey. At that humble church, Camiglia encountered a joy she had never experienced before. She found what her soul was thirsty for. That night, she and Joey found Christ as their personal Savior.

Camiglia's life immediately began to change. She had peace. Her heart was filled with joy. She found hope and unconditional love in the arms of the Savior. She had the calm assurance that God was guiding her life. She looked forward to every opportunity to worship the One who loved her and gave His life for her.

Benedetto loved his wife, and although he was not interested in church himself, he was supportive of her endeavors to follow Jesus. But Benny didn't understand why his wife would go to that little storefront church in Downtown Brooklyn and come back three hours later. It used to be only 45 minutes when she worshipped around the corner. One day, Benny told his wife, "You're not going to church. I'm going, and if I don't like it, you're not going back." He informed her that he suspected she had a lover at the church. Camiglia responded, "I do! And I want you to meet Him!"

Benny went to church that very night. The men met him at the door, shook his hand, and planted a kiss on his cheek saying, "Pace, fratello!" (Peace, brother!). He thought it was a password and he was upset that his wife didn't give him the password to get in! He stayed for the service and, of course, came home three hours later.

Benny arrived home and walked to his bedroom. A few moments later, he walked into the living room where his wife had been praying the entire time he was gone. She asked, "How did you like it?" His eyes filled with tears as he responded, *"Why didn't you tell me Jesus is this good?"*

That night, Benedetto Grassano heard Christ Jesus call him by name. He met Camiglia's "Lover." His eyes were opened, his heart was transformed, and a peace he had never experienced flooded his soul. In a literal New Testament conversion that we all too often miss today, salvation came into his life and changed everything. Not only did salvation come, but also the anointed touch of the Holy

Spirit and a call to preach God's Word. The family would never be the same.

Though I never met my grandfather (he died before my father married), the stories of his faith and God's favor on the family inspired me from a young age. God provided through miracles for the family, including my grandfather having a job through the Depression years. He left cement work when he acquired a job with the NYC Parks Department on 120th Street in Upper Manhattan and later in Prospect Park, Brooklyn.

He loved his job and was proud of his uniform. He would walk the park and pray. When he was on breaks, he would often kneel behind bushes to spend time alone with His Savior.

Benedetto became ill and was diagnosed with cancer. My father's youngest brother broke his leg, sending him to the same hospital where Benedetto was under care.

Without his salary, things became tight and food was scarce. Nevertheless, Camiglia informed her children, "We are going to church. There is no money even for food, but the Lord is real, and He will provide for us."

When they came home from church, there was a large box of groceries at their door. A note in the box said, "We don't know if you need this or not, but while we were on our knees praying, the Holy Spirit talked to us and we feel this is the will of God."

No one knew about the need in the home, only the Heavenly Father.

One Sunday, the pastor shared that the church funds were not sufficient to pay the church's rent. He asked for the congregation to give a special offering. Camiglia gave knowing that she would not have enough for her own rent, which was due the next day. She came home from church and spent time in prayer. Not feeling well, she almost chose not to return to the Sunday evening service, but she went nonetheless. At church that night, a godly couple came to

Nana and said, "This afternoon while in prayer, the Lord told us to give this to you."

They handed Camiglia an envelope. After church in the apartment, she opened it, and inside was the exact amount she needed to pay her rent. Only the Father knew about the need. God provided for His children. He always does. *"I have never seen the godly abandoned or their children begging for bread"* (Psalm 37:25).

Faith did not come without sacrifice for my grandparents. After her conversion, Nana's parents and siblings rejected her, cut her out of their will, and evicted the family from the home they were living in which was owned by her parents. Her father told her, "You have disgraced us by changing your religion. Therefore, you can no longer live in our home." My father was a young teen at the time. After receiving the eviction notice, Papa Benedetto borrowed a truck and began loading up their belongings to find a new place to live. While loading the truck, Nana's parents came.

"I don't know what's wrong with you, Camiglia," they said. "You have disgraced our family. I went to that place you call a church. It's a store-front building with folding chairs and a concrete floor. How could you leave the beauty of this cathedral for that place you call a church? What's the matter with you? Have you gone crazy?"

Nana responded, "It's true. Your church has a beauty that pleases the eyes, but my church has a beauty that pleases the soul."

That *beauty that pleases the soul* called my grandfather into ministry. Four of the five children were either called to or married into ministry. Papa would come home from work each night and pray for hours in his room, calling out to God for the needs of his family, friends, and church, and thanking God for His mercy and grace in their lives. He prayed for the men and women that his children would marry. He prayed for his grandchildren. That means he prayed for me.

On his deathbed, my father asked his father if it was truly worth serving Jesus after the rejection of family and the sickness he had endured. He looked into my father's eyes and responded with the words of an old hymn, "Sonny, it truly gets sweeter as the days go by." After sharing those words, he began to praise the Lord. He passed from earth to heaven in that moment.

Their church eventually rented a Jewish synagogue not far from their apartment for their Sunday services. There, in front of the Torah at 17 years old, God called my father to preach His Word and follow Him. He began as an evangelist holding successful revivals in the Mid-Atlantic and Southeast. In God's providence, he was invited to minister in South Carolina where he met my mother. They evangelized, pastored, built their first church, and led state youth and discipleship ministry for their denomination. When I was three years old, they moved to Detroit to pastor a church on a gravel road beside railroad tracks. It was there that I encountered the God of my fathers and chose to follow Him.

In over 60 years of ministry, God took my father to 70 nations. Fifty-one churches were planted. Church buildings were built in and outside the U.S. Missionaries have been encouraged, trained, sent to the field and supported. Young men were mentored and commissioned into ministry by my father, including the writer of this book. Only God knows what is in store for my children and others that will be influenced because of this heritage of faith.

Lidia and I had the privilege to disciple a young couple, Neil and Jennifer Lawrence, while I was teaching at Florida State University and completing my dissertation. My father was instrumental in sending Neil and Jennifer to fulfill their calling in Kenya and surrounding nations. In speaking of their mission in Africa, Neil said, *"Because of your dad and mom ministering to us, our students from many countries in Africa are multiplying the blessings to thousands of people. Truly, your parents' reward is great in heaven. There is a voice from Africa blessing them and acknowledging their life's work."*

This is the way things happen in the kingdom of God. Christ influences one through us. That one will influence another, who will influence another, andyet another. This is how we change the world.

Our faith foundation is deep on both sides of our family. Lidia's father heard the call of God as a young man in Chile and went to an unreached part of Paraguay with the Gospel. Through much opposition and many challenges, his persevering faith in God resulted in churches being planted in Paraguay, Northern Argentina, Southern Brazil, Uruguay, Chile and Guatemala. The churches that he planted grew and became church-planting churches, causing the Gospel to penetrate entire regions. They suffered persecution for their faith. They endured a Socialist government, earthquakes, civil war, and communities bound with witchcraft and demon worship. Through every struggle and trial, they saw that *"You intended to harm me, but God intended it all for good. He brought me to this position so I could save the lives of many people"* (Genesis 50:20).

God called us to follow Him, a calling rooted in the foundation of a heritage of faith that is now alive in our generation. Our families walked with God. We chose to walk with Him, and to follow Him to the places where He was preparing people to receive His hope.

My parents became the spiritual grandparents of our spiritual family at Harvest. The people called them "Mother Grassano" and "Father Grassano." They were blessed by the heritage of faith and the testimonies of God's faithfulness in my parents' walk with Christ, the very same testimonies that have inspired me.

Psalm 68:5-6 says that God is a *"father to the fatherless"* and *"God places the lonely into families."* The people God was changing in the South Bronx did not have families like Lidia and I had. God had grafted them into a spiritual family where not only He became a father to the fatherless, but where faithful followers of Christ became examples to the life of faith and living testimonies to the faithfulness of God.

These followers of Christ at Harvest began a new heritage of faith for themselves and their children. A new generation is learning and experiencing that walking with Jesus is the beauty that pleases their souls.

---

[1] *Christ Stopped at Eboli,* Carlo Levi. Farrar, Straus and Company, 1947. Page 4.

Chapter Fourteen

A Deeper Valley

"I will never fail you. I will never abandon you."

Hebrews 13:5

We faced intense forms of spiritual warfare from the beginning of our work in the South Bronx. There was never a week that we were not dealing with crises of physical abuse, sexual abuse, addictions, violence, financial struggles, facility issues, witchcraft and more. These things kept us close to the cross, a blessed and safe place to be.

In September 2004, many new teenagers joined our youth ministry through our summer outreaches. Working closely with our youth leadership team (mostly college-aged young adults whom Lidia and I were mentoring), we decided to have an all-night fellowship with these new teens at *The Harvest Center*. We began about 7:00 p.m. with refreshments, followed by games, a student-led sharing time, and opportunities for our leaders to get to know these new youth. There were about 45 of us present.

At 11:00 p.m., we gathered in a circle for a Bible study. I chose Ephesians 6:10-18 to share with these youth about the provision God gives us to face opposition. Opposition has always been fierce in our community, and I knew they would face it very early in their walk with the Lord. They would need to rely on God and put on His armor to stand firm.

After 15 minutes of sharing, one of the new girls asked, "Is Satan really real?" I began to answer with scriptures, but I was interrupted with a knock on the door, which was odd this late at night. Lidia saw who it was and cautioned me to take one of the young men to the door with me, so I did.

I opened the door and said hello. The people lunged forward and began to assault me, hitting me in the head and body and then knocking me to the floor where they began to kick me. Raul, Cephas and Junior quickly jumped into action to pull them off me and push them out the door. One of our youth leaders grabbed my children, Angel and Tommy, and ran to the bathroom, locking the door behind them. Angel was a young teen and Tommy was almost six years old. Inside the bathroom, that youth leader began to pray as she guarded the door with my children inside. I am grateful to her to this day.

With the assailants pushed out the door, we assessed the damage to the facility and to me. A hole in the wall resulted from the struggle to push one of them out the door. Other than bruises mostly on my face, head and side, I was fine.

Someone called the police and, in a fashion rare in our community, they arrived quickly. When they realized that one of the assailants was an off-duty cop, internal affairs and his precinct captain were called.

I went downstairs to my office to pray. I asked the Lord for direction. This was a situation I had never experienced. The Lord reminded me of David in a cave with the opportunity to bring judgment on Saul. David chose to wait and leave it in the hands of the Lord. I chose to do the same. The internal affairs officer and the precinct captain tried to convince me to press charges. I would not. I knew the people and loved them. I chose to leave them and the situation in God's hands.

God promises that He will take what was meant for evil and turn it into good. I wondered how God would do that with this situation.

We saw evidence of it in the new teens who witnessed the assault. They had never seen people not fight back. The South Bronx has its own form of justice. Retribution is always carried out. We protected ourselves as best we could and removed the problem, but we did not fight back. I chose not to fight back in bringing charges against them. These teens saw a different approach from the street justice that they knew. God has a better way.

I was sore the following day, but Lidia and my hearts hurt the most. These words became very real: *"Trust in the Lord with all your heart; do not depend on your own understanding. Seek His will in all you do, and He will show you which path to take"* (Proverbs 3:5-6).

As we entered *The Harvest Center* for Sunday worship, the people looked intently at us, almost as if they were studying us and awaiting our response. We tried to act as normal as possible, as though nothing had happened. I chose to share on unconditional forgiveness that day.

There were different reactions from the people who knew us. When the guys on the street learned about the assault, they pressed me to know who did it. This did not happen in one conversation, but for over three years. I could not tell them who it was, for I knew what could happen to those people. I would not allow that blood to be on my hands.

Our spiritual family at Harvest waited to see what our response would be. They were anticipating us announcing that we were leaving the Bronx. There would be no such announcement. After they saw that we were not going anywhere, they began to rise up as never before, taking the responsibility and leadership for which we had prayed and labored. That was a blessing.

I shared with a small circle of intercessors about the event. Their prayers became a great source of encouragement. Over and over again, I would be reminded that people were praying: a phone call from Alaska, a phone call from a denominational leader who became a faithful intercessor, a message from Christian artist David

Crowder that his intercessors were praying for us. (I had met David early in his career and often prayed for him.) These and others provided heartfelt encouragement. We were not alone. God and His servants were standing with us.

I tried to keep the assault from my parents. I did not want to add the extra worry to their burden for us. I accidentally included them in a prayer update to intercessors. Mom and Dad called, asking, "Son, is there something you need to tell us?" I knew what they meant and informed them in detail about what had taken place. They took the position they had always taken of prayerful concern for their children and grandchildren while trusting God for the best.

There was pressure from our Board of Directors for us to leave. In a meeting after the assault, the board decided that it was time for us to go. There was only one objection. Interestingly, that objection was my father. He posed this question: "What about the church? Who will lead these people?" He cared deeply for us, and he cared deeply for God's people.

Lidia sat with me as I responded to the Board: "I wrote into the by-laws of this ministry organization that I would be under your authority. If this is truly your decision, we must comply, but I have one question. Are you making this decision because the Lord has so directed you, or out of concern for our safety? For if it is out of concern for our safety, remember that the safest place for us to be is in the middle of God's plan for us." One by one the board members shared that their decision was for our safety, which I appreciated. I appreciated most of all their increased commitment to pray for us as we continued to follow the heart of God for the South Bronx community He had placed us in.

As a result of this event, I became much closer to Gerson. Gerson, called Junior, was one of our young leaders. He was an exceptionally kind young man, loved by absolutely everyone. He had a heart wide open for God to fill, and God was certainly filling it with His love, His mercy and His truth. Junior and I were always close, but after the assault, he would meet me at a train station in Manhattan and take the train with me to the Bronx. If I were driving, he would call me to know when I was arriving and wait for me to park so he could walk with me to the church. Junior worked faithfully with the children's ministry, drama ministry, and youth ministry. He also volunteered to clean the church.

Junior shared his heart more and more with me through our increased time together. We shared about scriptures, about God's love for the people of our community, and about God's love for him. He came to me in the middle of September informing me that God had confirmed a call to ministry. We were close before, but we became so much closer in that mentoring relationship.

The crises did not stop that September. The Harvest Center flooded three times with raw sewage. The NYC Health Department threatened to shut us down. Our insurance was canceled. Our landlord informed us that they would evict us if we had no insurance. We finally found insurance for three times the cost. We had two accidents in our van. We learned that my daughter, Angel, would need spinal fusion surgery for scoliosis. My father's health began to weaken. We were living the expression, "When it rains, it pours."

I traveled to my parents in South Carolina to help them with some work on their house. Some men from a local church were to assist me. I invited Junior to speak to the youth at Harvest that Friday night. Everyone reported to me that he did an excellent job sharing from 1 Corinthians 13 about the unconditional love of God for us that we should have for one another.

Junior was honored to speak to the youth. He made a strangely funny remark afterwards, saying, "I could die now and be happy. I've done everything I ever wanted to do with my life." His birthday was only eight days away. One of the women mentioned his birthday, and Junior said, "I don't know why, but I never thought I would make it to my 21st birthday."

The next morning, I was working in the yard of my parent's home with the men from a local church. As I was sharing with the pastor about the things we had been enduring, I said, "God is faithful, but I don't know how we can carry much more." At that very moment, my mother came running to me with the phone. She was distraught. I took the phone and heard my wife's broken voice. With tears of deep sorrow, she informed me that Junior was dead. It was October 2, 2004, one month after the assault in the church.

We had a mentoring ministry in the Bronx giving the opportunity for the men and young men of Harvest to pour into the teenage boys. This day was a bike ride. While riding down East 149th Street, Junior's bike was hit from behind, throwing him off his bike and under a delivery truck passing by. He was killed instantly in the full view of the men and boys that were with them.

I arranged a flight to return quickly to the Bronx. The plane was half empty, which thankfully gave me a row to myself allowing me to pour my heart out to God and plead for mercy. Behind me sat a group of Jamaicans returning from a mission trip. As the plane took off, they began to sing hymns of praise. I realized that God, in His mercy, had placed them there. I left my seat and introduced myself to them. I informed them of what had happened that morning. We prayed and sang together for most of that flight.

All these events brought me to the end of myself. I didn't know how we could carry much more. God became very real, even more than before, and the vision remained to see change in the community. I was broken as never before. The questions of my heart poured out to God:

"God, what can you show me about You through all of this? How can I make sense of all these things? I am weak and broken. Please give me the strength to keep walking! What yet must change in me? What part of my flesh is yet to be co-crucified with You?" These and other questions poured forth from my heart daily. He graciously gave us the strength for each new day.

Then the trials began to hit home. The next few years would bring more tears as we walked into unknown places with much greater dependence on God.

We took my daughter to three spinal specialists. The first two gave us their opinions: my daughter needed spinal fusion surgery. Her scoliosis had reached the stage that surgery was mandatory. Not only was there a curvature of the spine, but the spine was also twisting between the shoulders.

Angel had worn an uncomfortable prosthetic brace for over three years. It did nothing to correct or prevent further curvature. By God's divine providence, an "out of the blue" phone call from Dan Buttafuoco, the father of a former classmate of Angel, resulted in a referral to one of the top pediatric spinal surgeons in the Northeast. The doctor was in no hurry to operate. If necessary, he would use the newest techniques, minimizing some of the difficult aspects of recuperation.

Many were praying for Angel. Some, in a sincere desire for her to be prevented from experiencing this surgery, shared with us their belief that surgery would not be necessary. They said there would be a miraculous healing. I wanted to believe that, but something in my spiritual gut told me it was not true.

I wrestled with the prospect of my precious daughter going through this surgical procedure. It would take two years or more for full recuperation. She was a sophomore in high school. I just didn't want to see that happen for her. I struggled with the potential surgery and constantly brought my daughter to the Lord in prayer, pleading for another way.

Driving home one night from *The Harvest Center*, the Spirit of the Lord spoke to me while crossing the Throgs Neck Bridge, "Are you willing for Me to heal her through surgery?" I could not answer.

I believe that God uses many methods of healing. Sometimes healing is through miraculous divine intervention. God is certainly able to do that, as He often does. Other times God heals through those whom He has given the abilities to do surgery and other medical treatments. Sometimes He allows us to walk through valleys to accomplish eternal purposes in our lives and in the lives of others.

It took me two weeks to answer the Lord's question. Eventually, I said yes. I was willing for God to heal through surgery.

Two of the most difficult nights and days of my life were the night before and the day of Angel's surgery. Lidia and I barely slept a wink, praying all night long. Seeing her rolled into the operating room was heart wrenching. The surgery lasted almost six hours and was successful. Her spine was straightened. Titanium rods were screwed into her vertebrae keeping her back straight. Angel now boasts that, while she is barely five feet tall, she is the only one among all her friends who grew nearly three inches in six hours.

After the surgery in ICU, we heard what we thought was Angel moaning in pain. Lidia came close to her face and heard Angel singing, *"Jesus loves me this I know…"* Angel doesn't remember singing it, but the song was in her heart. Later in recovery, she began to sing *"Remember Your people. Remember Your children. Remember Your promise, O Lord. Your grace is enough…"* She doesn't remember that either.

We brought her home after nearly a week in the hospital. We had to turn Angel every 15 minutes 24 hours a day for a couple weeks to rotate her position. She had to learn to do many things again: sit up, walk, tie her shoes, get dressed. She was taking honors and A.P. classes at the time. After the first stage of her recuperation, teachers came to the house. She excelled in all her classes. She aggressively approached physical rehab, doing it at a rehab center used by the New York Islanders. Being the hockey fans that we are, I believe this may have provided even more inspiration for her hard work at recovery.

Angel's surgery became a defining moment in her life and in her faith. Part of the reason she is the strong woman of God that she is today is because of that experience. After fifteen months, completely amazed at her progress, her surgeon released her to full physical activity. To her mother's chagrin, she asked the surgeon if she could learn to play ice hockey. He said yes. She did.

Less than a year after Angel's surgery, my mother had a heart attack and my father's health began to fail. Mom recovered from her heart attack, but Dad did not improve. My dear father's health began to decline. He was misdiagnosed by doctors which delayed proper treatment. Eventually, it reached the place that Dad could no longer be at home, which as many know is a terribly difficult decision. There were many times that my father would cry out in pain for an entire day, or two, until nurses gave enough pain meds to knock him out for a couple days. Sometimes the only thing that would calm him and ease his pain was when Angel would hold his hand and sing to him. The entire experience ripped at our hearts, watching a man of such dignity decline in this manner and endure such hardship. It was heart breaking.

During that same time, our finances tanked. We were, and we remain today, a faith ministry that relies solely on the generosity of people whose monthly partnership enables us to do this work among the poor and disenfranchised. When economic hardship hits the country, charitable giving declines. We were among many who felt the effects of this in significant ways, resulting in little or no salary for months at a time. We endured constant flooding with raw sewage in our offices and library at *The Harvest Center* with no funds to do the needed repairs. Through it all, the people at Harvest had such a love for God and one another that it would not deter from the joy of what Jesus was doing in their lives. Eventually, we acquired insurance and we continue to minister through that facility today.

Dad always taught me that family is first. I don't ever remember him teaching me this with words. He lived it before me. He and Mom were there for me throughout my life. I have wonderful memories of Dad coming home from the office, rolling up his sleeves, tucking his tie into his shirt, and then grabbing his baseball glove to play catch with me until it was so dark we could hardly see the ball. It was now my time to live the same, placing family and honoring parents above all else.

Making one of the most difficult decisions of our lives, with the full support of our board, we sold our parsonage. God had provided this place for us to live in 1998 through a generous and miraculous gift from a godly man in Charlotte. We purchased it as a carpenter's special significantly under market price. It needed a new roof, new siding, new electrical, and the interior needed to be redone. We took five years to do the repairs and upgrades with the help of volunteer contractors, carpenters and electricians. It was a comfortable home a short drive to *The Harvest Center*.

The house did not stay on the market very long, but then we encountered another battle. In the state of New York, the sale of any property owned by a not-for-profit had to be approved by the attorney general and the State Board of Appeals. Our attorney general had just been elected governor and had released communication that all applications would be tabled for the next attorney general who would take office in a few months. Our buyers were not happy and threatened to pull out of the contract. We were running out of funds and desperately needed to close.

On the Monday before Thanksgiving, Tim Barnes, my college roommate from Furman University, called me. We had not spoken in years. Tim was coming to New York City. He had heard about our ministry and wanted to see us. At the end of the phone call, Tim asked how he could pray for us. I shared with him about this situation and about how desperate it was becoming. We needed a miracle.

Then Tim said words that revealed the power and providence of God yet again. The governor-elect of the State of New York was the brother-in-law of a deacon in his church in North Carolina. The governor's sister-in-law worked in the cubicle beside Tim's wife at her job. Tim said, "Tom, this is God. Let me make a phone call."

Tim called me back late that evening with the email address of the sister-in-law of the governor elect. She asked me to send all the details about our ministry and about the urgent situation needing closure on the parsonage. I compiled the information and sent everything to her that Wednesday afternoon, the day before Thanksgiving.

Our lawyer called me the Monday after Thanksgiving a little after 9:00 a.m. The attorney general's office had called him asking for detailed information about our work, including a daily schedule of our activities. We sent the information to them that afternoon.

The following morning, our lawyer called me again. The attorney general's office had called him informing him that our application had been approved and that we were exempt from the remainder of the application process. They said, "You can schedule your closing." Yet another great miracle of our great God had taken place.

On the home front, things did not improve. Dad's health continued to fail. He was eventually diagnosed with Shy-Drager Syndrome (now called Multiple System Atrophy), a neurological disease resulting from degeneration of nerve cells in the brain and spinal cord. Dad died in July of 2009. His funeral was attended by church leaders and missionaries from around the world. Among the speakers was Dr. Lamar Vest, the President of the American Bible Society whom Dad had mentored when he was a teen, along with leaders of the denomination that was home to my father's ministry. It was, truly, a beautiful and inspiring homecoming.

Dad carried the cross with dignity and integrity and influenced thousands to follow Christ. But he was my dad. My pastor. My mentor. My best friend. He was the man that was always there for every concert and every sports event. Family was always first. He was the man that held up a standard and believed in what I could become if I put my faith in God, worked hard and made right choices. He was the man that, while concerned about my family and especially his granddaughter, was among the few who, along with my mother, supported my decision to leave all that I knew and to go the Bronx. I am so profoundly thankful for my father.

The tragedies continued to come. Months after my father's death, my aunt died of cancer. Several months after that, the girl of my dreams, my wife Lidia, was diagnosed with cancer.

A cancer diagnosis is difficult for anyone to accept. There is a sort of denial at first. At least that's what I had. I wanted to fight against the diagnosis. One morning at breakfast, Lidia and I talked through everything. We prayed together and an overwhelming peace was present in our hearts. We were so thankful. As we got up from the breakfast table, the phone rang. It was the doctor. They found more cancer. Surgery would be more extensive than we thought.

I embraced my wife and failed terribly to hide my emotions as tears welled up in my eyes. I assured her God was with her, I was with her, and everything would be okay. Then I walked into my office attached to our house and yelled at God, "I do not doubt who You are, but I cannot find You in this! Where are You?" He was silent, but I knew He was still there.

He was present through the two years of three surgeries. Lidia's cancer was found in the initial stage. Her oncologist informed us it could be called "Cancer Level Zero." The diagnosis was truly a miracle. Many other doctors would not have found it, but her doctor did. Though the two years of surgeries were difficult, God saw us through, and my beautiful wife is well.

The funds from the sale of the parsonage began to run dry. Giving did not increase. I was forced, one by one, to lay off staff. We sacrificed salary to stretch the dwindling finances as much as we could. Laying off staff eventually meant shutting down vital programs. With all we had endured to establish the work, this was incredibly painful, but there was nothing else that we could do. Yet again God proved His Word. Jesus said, *"Upon this rock I will build My church and the powers of hell will not conquer it"* (Matthew 16:18).

God raised up leaders in the Bronx and the work in Detroit grew exponentially with a volunteer force. The ministry never ceased.

A month after Lidia's first surgery, a dear aunt died suddenly and unexpectedly. Then Lidia's father's health began to fail. My father-in-law died in July 2013, four years after my father's death. Both men died in the middle of our summer outreach. Though small in stature, my father-in-law was a giant of faith. The entire region of a continent was influenced because of how he walked with God. He was a man of deep passion for souls and compassion for the suffering. He held a high standard just by his walk with Christ. He and I became quite close after my father's passing. I miss him deeply.

After my father-in-law passed, another aunt died. Five family deaths in a little over five years. Then came news that I was not expecting.

A dear friend pressed upon me to get life insurance. I finally succumbed and began the process. The physical revealed something irregular with my heart. A heart sonogram followed, and then a transesophageal ultrasound after that. That is where they saw it clearly. I had a severely failing heart valve.

The strange thing about this was that I had no symptoms. Doctors were astonished that I didn't. They said I shouldn't have been able to walk 50 yards or climb one flight of stairs without being out of breath. I was helping coach my son's hockey team. I always skated laps with the players, yet I had no symptoms. To test myself, I tried walking up six flights of stairs to see what would happen. I did it four times with a 30 second break on the top each time. I did not become winded, but I did have very sore calves the next day!

Here we were again, facing an unexpected diagnosis and impending surgery.

During Dad's sickness, I met a man named Jim. Jim worked with the Detroit Red Wings. He became a dear friend, and our families became close. Jim would call me or text me every week during the final year of Dad's suffering to check on me. He and his family were there for us before, during and after Dad's passing. Jim's wife Bekki, a cancer survivor herself, was a strength, encouragement and support to Lidia during her treatment.

Jim called me the day after my diagnosis. He had me on his mind. (How often we have seen God do that!) I informed him of my diagnosis. He said, "Tom, let me call you right back."

Jim called me back in 20 minutes. He had called the Red Wings team doctor. "When are you going to Detroit?" Jim asked. I was leaving for Detroit in two days. He asked me to take my medical records. "Doc" would meet me when I arrived.

And he did. The team doctor met us at our hotel. We conversed for a while. He took my medical records to two friends of his who specialize in cardiothoracic surgery. They recommended Dr. Doug Murphy at Emory-St. Joseph Hospital in Atlanta. What I did not know at the time was that Dr. Murphy was the innovator of the robotic heart valve repair. Although Dr. Murphy was internationally renowned and difficult to get an appointment with, I called and secured an appointment the next day. Instead of having traditional heart surgery, I would have nickel-sized incisions on my side. The robotic arms would cut into the back of my heart and repair my valve rather than replacing it. I would be on the heart-lung machine one third of the time of traditional surgery.

While avoiding surgery by miraculous intervention would have been preferable, I saw the hand of God clearly in every step: suffering from no symptoms, being diagnosed despite no symptoms, and having the surgical procedure that I had with the internationally renowned surgeon Dr. Doug Murphy.

While we hoped for a cessation to what was now ten years of hospitals and funeral homes, that did not happen. After more than two years of suffering in pain during which my mother was misdiagnosed and not treated correctly, she was accurately diagnosed with a cancerous tumor around her pelvis. Doctors had been treating her for radiating pain from spinal degeneration.

The treatment was much more successful than the oncologists ever would have imagined. My mother's pain decreased to about 10 percent of what it had been, and her quality of life returned. Her oncologist admitted this exceeded his expectations and shared how ecstatic he was with the results of her treatment.

The last weekend of April of 2017, we went shopping with my mother. She bought some new clothes and shoes. We were all so happy and enjoyed a meal of celebration together. A few days later, Mom had a stroke. Mom had atrial fibrillation, an irregular and often rapid heartbeat that requires being medicated with blood thinners to reduce the risk of stroke. A couple of days after Mom's stroke we learned that the nurses at her care facility failed to administer Mom's blood thinners for almost two weeks. Her stroke was the result.

This news was harder to swallow because of the successful cancer treatment and the return of her quality of life. Moms' resilience did not wane. She worked hard at rehab and bounced back in many areas, though never regaining her ability to swallow. She died in January of 2018 from aspirational pneumonia.

A pastor's wife from New York City described my mother well: *"A gentle spirit of meekness, poised with grace and humility, yet filled with power and conviction."*

Mom was 93 years old when she died, but she looked twenty years younger. No one could believe her age. She led an amazing life, supporting and encouraging my father and gifted herself as a Bible teacher and pastor's wife. She lost her mother to typhoid fever when she was two years old. She and her three-month-old sister went to live with her grandmother. Her baby sister died three months later, and then her grandmother died. Her 16-year-old Aunt Mary took her in and became her mother.

When her father remarried years later, he brought her home, but her stepmother never accepted her. The only love of a mother she ever experienced was through her Aunt Mary. Her stepmother even opposed her father being in her wedding and giving her away.

A cousin did it instead. This is why my mother often said, "My life began when I met your father." Not having a mother engaged in her life or in her wedding was the reason she took such great joy being involved in our wedding and loving my wife as her own daughter.

My mother had difficulty conceiving. She lost children prematurely. She endured years of fertility treatment and finally became pregnant with me nearly 15 years into their marriage. She almost died when I was born and could have no more children. Our family had always been close, and her loss left a void, yet a deep gratitude for the incredible, loving champions of faith that I had the honor of calling Mom and Dad.

In a little more than 12 years, our family endured my daughter's spinal surgery, my mother's heart attack, my father's illness and death, the passing of three aunts, my wife's cancer, my father-in-law's illness and death, my heart surgery, deep financial crisis, and my mother's passing.

Many people say that suffering proves there is no God. Not to me. Suffering proves there is suffering in a sinful and fallen world. When we turn our eyes to Jesus in the midst of the storms, He proves His amazing love, His strength in our weaknesses, His light in our darkness, His power to face and overcome our suffering, and His Lordship over everything. He proves His faithfulness. He gives us hope in every situation. He proves He is God.

During the years of sickness, struggle and death that seemed like they would never end, God continued to bless. A new group of servant leaders were raised up at *The Harvest Center.* They are faithfully fulfilling the vision of Urban Harvest, serving as God's instruments to change lives and to bring hope to our community. This includes Lesly Exil, born in an area of Haiti influenced by voodoo, this new creation in Christ faithfully serves as shepherd of the spiritual sheep at Harvest, along with his wonderful family. It includes Maurice Salley, who spent 17 years as an addict on the streets. His story of redemption is miraculous and inspiring. He is exceptionally gifted in sharing the Gospel, passionate about the Great Commission, and a leader in evangelism in the South Bronx. His transformed life serves as a light and witness to all those around him. It also includes Alexandra and Andre, Willie and Shami, Vonetta, Angel, Sharon, Cathy, Christian and many others whose lives intersected with His grace and who now effectively extend God's hands of mercy and love to others.

In Detroit, *Hope for the City* grew in influence and scope, touching many communities in the city, reaching thousands of souls with the hope of the Gospel, and changing the spiritual DNA of churches from inward focus to effectively bringing Jesus to the doorsteps of the people in the streets around them. God has opened new doors to the nations and to immigrant people groups in the city. *"The faithful love of the LORD never ends! His mercies never cease. Great is His faithfulness"* (Lamentations 3:22-23).

As I look back at a quarter of a century of serving, loving, following God and standing steadfastly by His grace with this ministry, I see my greatest vision and desire has come true: the truth of the gospel has become relevant, alive, and cherished in our children. My daughter Angel and my son Tommy have experienced many of the stories in this book with Lidia and me. We believe God called our family to serve Him, and so we have, together. The years of struggle and suffering drew my children closer to the Lord. They have seen that the Savior we serve is as alive today as He was in scripture. They have chosen to follow Him, not because of us, but because of who He has become to each of them. This is our greatest treasure.

There was a passage of scripture, among many, that came to mean much to me during the latter part of those years of storms. It is found in 2 Corinthians 4:7-9; 13-16.

"We now have this light shining in our hearts, but we ourselves are like fragile clay jars containing this great treasure. This makes it clear that our great power is from God, not from ourselves.

"We are pressed on every side by troubles, but we are not crushed. We are perplexed, but not driven to despair. We are hunted down, but never abandoned by God. We get knocked down, but we are not destroyed … But we continue to preach because we have the same kind of faith the psalmist had when he said, "I believed in God, so I spoke."

"We know that God, who raised the Lord Jesus, will also raise us with Jesus and present us to Himself together with you. All of this is for your benefit. And as God's grace reaches more and more people, there will be great thanksgiving, and God will receive more and more glory.

"That is why we never give up."

Yes, that is why we never give up.

When all around us appears to have no beauty, when there is little that is appealing in our eyes, there can still be a beauty in our souls, a sustaining force we cannot explain nor comprehend that leads us through the storms to brighter seas and peaceful shores where we realize we are much stronger than before.

God does bring beauty from ashes. In every situation we encounter, Jesus will walk with us, closely by our side. We may not always sense His presence, but He is there, covering us with His loving protection, pouring out the grace we need for each struggle that we face. We may walk through valleys, but we are never alone; our Lord is always with us.

"For I have chosen you and will not throw you away. Don't be afraid, for I am with you. Don't be discouraged, for I am your God. I will strengthen you and help you. I will hold you up with My victorious right hand" (Isaiah 41:9-10).

Chapter Fifteen

Vietnam

"He had to go through Samaria."

John 4:4

I was born in the sixties. Those were difficult times of cultural crisis and war along with great advancements of culture, science and technology. I remember as a young child watching man's first steps on the moon. Vietnam was in the news every night, and this nation grabbed my heart during those years. Part of the reason for that was Bruce Marsee.

Bruce was my buddy, sort of my hero. When I was a child in Michigan, Bruce would play with me and carry me on his shoulders. I would watch him singing in the youth choir and then scoot to the edge of the pew so he could pinch or tickle me as he walked down from the choir loft.

I was nine years old when Bruce enlisted. His brother Curt, and Danny, another young man from the church, went to Southeast Asia as well. I sat in front of the TV every night watching the vivid war reports and newscasts from the front lines, praying for Bruce to come home safely. The images of the Vietnamese people, the children, the napalm, the intense pain of war, the young soldiers, and the devastation of a nation made an everlasting impact on my young life.

I was excited when my mother told me Bruce was home and was coming to church that Sunday morning. I ran through the halls of the church until I found him standing in the hallway by the doors to the sanctuary. Bruce stared at me with a hollow, empty look. He was back, but not all of him. I didn't see Bruce very much after that day. We moved from Michigan a few years later, but I never forgot Bruce.

My burden for Vietnam grew to the point I knew that I had to go. The problem was that nobody was going during that time. I called denominational and parachurch mission organizations and short-term mission agencies around the nation to learn about what God was doing in Vietnam, but I found no one with knowledge or experience there. By God's providence, I met the leader of a ministry of Vietnam veterans that was conducting reconciliation trips and medical clinics in Vietnam. God gave me the opportunity to go.

My first trip to Vietnam was nearly 25 years after the last time I saw Bruce. I wanted to contact him before my departure. My mother was able to acquire Bruce's phone number from a woman from my father's former pastorate in Metro Detroit who knew Bruce's mom.

I called Bruce and gave my name. He said, "Well, I haven't heard that name in a while!" We shared about old times and rekindled a relationship. I informed him that I was going to Vietnam. I told him I prayed for him every day while he was there, and I asked him to pray for me. He obliged.

While on the flight, I recorded the following in my journal: "I spoke to Bruce last Saturday. As I began to share about how I prayed for him and what I am doing now, he broke down and cried. He shared things he said neither my parents nor his knew. I shared with him about my trip to Vietnam. Now he is praying for me. Somehow I know I will see Bruce again."

I encountered the hand of God every day of the three weeks I was "in country," beginning the day of my arrival. I flew from New York City to Frankfurt to Singapore. After another lay-over, I took a short flight to Saigon, called Ho Chi Minh City since 1975. It took more than 30 hours of flight time. I was finally there.

Tan Son Nhat Airport was a little more intimidating in 1996 than it is now. There were anti-aircraft guns around the tarmac and Russian-made MiG's parked in front of hangers at the airport. Flight attendants informed us on the final flight that we had to declare newspapers, books, recorded tapes, electronics, and all cultural information that we were bringing into the country. I had all the above, many of them items to distribute with followers of The Way while I was there. I filled in the customs forms with the purposes of each one as instructed: "books for reading, tapes for listening to," etc. Then I prayed, "Lord, lead me to the right customs agent."

The first stop after deplaning was to check visas. The government agent repeatedly asked me questions in Vietnamese that I could not answer. There was only one other American on the flight, a businessman, who could not help me. The agent forcefully stamped my visa and pointed to customs, angrily saying something I could not understand.

I entered the room where there were customs agents in small booths and armed military walking around. Every booth had a line of eight to ten people except one, which had no one. I proceeded to that booth.

In quite good English, the agent said, "Hello sir. Welcome to Vietnam!" He put his hand out for my customs form. When he saw it, he drew a loud, deep breath, and then took his pen and marked a large "X" across it. My heart sank. I had heard of people going to places like Vietnam and only seeing the airport to be turned around and sent back home.

The customs agent gave me a new form, leaned over his podium, and in a soft voice so that no one could hear, he said, "Only put video camera."

Feeling very surreal, I walked to a small countertop, filled out the new form, and then returned to the same custom agent. He greeted me as if he had never seen me before. "Hello sir. Welcome to Vietnam!" He reviewed my passport and visa, stamped my customs form, and then spoke to the guard who was now positioned near me. I do not know what he said, but as soon as he spoke, the guard did an 'about face' and never looked back at me.

The agent instructed me to place my bags on the belt for the x-ray machine and then ever-so-purposefully swept his forearm across his podium, knocking his papers onto the floor. He knelt down in no hurry whatsoever to pick them up. As a result, I was the only one looking at the monitor of the x-ray machine while my bags, with all their contents, were scanned. I knew God's merciful hand was at work.

I proceeded to retrieve my luggage and saw the large, intimidating crowd outside the door. I wondered how I would get through the crowd of people and find transportation to the hotel. As I was just about to grab my luggage, a young man came from the right, grabbed my bags, and in perfect English said, "Follow me, sir." I felt a very real peace and followed him.

Instead of walking through the doors into the large crowd, he took me down a hallway with airport, military and government offices on the right. He led me through this area as if we both belonged there. One man in uniform looked up from his desk with bewilderment on his face as he watched us walking by.

We exited a door at the end of the hallway and walked outside where a taxi was waiting with the trunk open. The young man put my luggage in the trunk and then asked me where I was going. I showed him the paper with the name of the hotel. He spoke to the driver in Vietnamese, opened the door of the taxi for me and said, "Have a nice stay in Vietnam, sir."

I checked into the hotel and met the other American on my flight. We walked around a bit and had dinner together. I learned he was a believer. When the rest of the team arrived near midnight, I approached the team leader and thanked him for having the young man there to secure my transportation. The leader said, "Tom, I don't know what you're talking about." In my first hour in Vietnam, God had already revealed His faithfulness.

Our trip took us through many areas of Vietnam, including Saigon, Da Nang, Huế, Đông Hà, Khe Sanh and others. Near Da Nang, we stayed in an area called Non Nuoc in a hotel that was built as a Soviet military R&R center. Just down the road were the Marble Mountains, a cluster of five hills made from limestone and marble. A centuries- old Buddhist shrine is located on the largest Marble Mountain and, on top of the highest peak, a spectacular view of China Beach.

Inside the mountain is a series of caves and pathways. The only Asian-American I met on the trip, a young lady with brown hair and freckles born in 1975, offered to be my guide. She spoke relatively good English. She took me through the shrine to an opening guarded by two hideous stone creatures. "These are the gatekeepers for the pathways to heaven and hell," she said. "First I will take you on the pathway to hell. Then I will take you on the pathway to heaven."

The similarities of these pathways to Jesus' words in Matthew 7:13-14 were remarkable: *"The highway to hell is broad, and its gate is wide for the many who choose that way. But the gateway to life is very narrow and the road is difficult …"* The pathway to hell on Marble Mountain was a wide inner pathway descending into a cave where more stone figures were present. Altars were in the pit of the cave with incense burning. I was told that this cave was a Viet Cong hospital and operations base during the war. At the very top of this cave, several stories high, was a small hole with a tiny ray of sunlight drawing you to a better place above this dark dwelling. After a few minutes there, my guide said, "Now I will take you on the pathway to heaven."

The pathway to heaven was not so easy. We ascended the mountain and found ourselves in a tiny space where we had to crawl up through a crevasse barely big enough for me to fit through. I had a backpack with my camera and a few other supplies that were preventing me from further progress. I had to unburden myself of my backpack and hand it up to my guide to make it through the crevasse. Just like my faith walk with Jesus, I have to give my burden to my Guide to make it to the place called heaven.

After passing through the crevasse, we found ourselves on the top of the largest of the Marble Mountains. The view was spectacular with rice patties on one side and the South China Sea on the other. We stayed there for a moment taking in the air and the view. Then I asked my guide, "In your religion, how do you get to heaven?"

I already knew the answer. I asked to begin a conversation about eternal things. I said, "In my faith …" and shared about our pathway to heaven. We continued to talk all the way down the mountain. A crowd of youth among whom a few spoke English began to walk with us. One teenage girl said she liked my hat. I put it on her head. She could not believe it. "You sure? You sure?" I assured her I was happy to give it to her. Then she gave me her hat as she said, "Thank you! Thank you! Thank you!"

While browsing the souvenir shops at the foot of the mountains, a lady asked, "Are you Brit? Swede? Russian? Where you from?" Not many Americans were traveling to Vietnam at this time. When I said, "American," she quickly invited me into her home, sat me at her humble table, introduced me to her husband and made some tea. Many of the youth I had met on Marble Mountain joined us. Among the sixteen youth were three who spoke English and translated as I answered questions about my country and asked them questions about their country.

I told them stories about the Living God. They had not heard of this before. Their faces and wide-opened eyes revealed the intense interest they had to learn more.

The woman had a marble sculpture that I wanted to purchase for my wife, but I did not have the $20 with me. I informed her I would come the next day, and I did. When I arrived, she again sat me at her table and fixed tea. She asked if I would wait for her so that she could go to the market to purchase a gift for my wife. While she went, I watched her husband make two bookends from a chunk of marble. He started with a large chisel and hammer banging away until the form began to take shape. He used a smaller chisel and hammer next, cutting the jagged edges of what was becoming horse-shaped bookends. Then he began to use a smaller but much sharper chisel to finish the details. I was fascinated, feeling like Jeremiah at the potter's wheel watching this man create beauty from a chunk of rock and chisel away the jagged edges until it reached perfection, just like the Great Sculptor does with you and me, if we allow Him.

As I was drinking my tea and taking in this experience, a teenage girl came and said, "Do you remember me?" I recognized her as one of the youth I had met the day before. She had read the Gospel story that I had given her and others. She wanted to learn more. As I sat with her, the woman and her husband, I felt as if the Holy Spirit took control of my words. I had never shared in this context before, much less at the foot of a sacred Buddhist shrine. I continually referred to the Father as the Living God. I shared why I believe in Him, about the things I have seen Him do, and about His love for all of them. The crowd grew until there were 18 Vietnamese, mostly teens, listening to testimony about the love of the Living God for them as four translated.

The teenage girl with whom I had traded hats the day before said, "I lied to you. I told you I like Americans. I don't like Americans. Americans killed my grandfather. They killed my uncle. I hate Americans. But I like you. You different. Why you different?" I explained the love of God in my heart in words she could understand.

I was deeply impacted by their absolute amazement of the revelation of a God who is alive, who loves them, who cares for every detail of their lives, who protects them and guides them, who speaks through His Book, who provides a pathway to eternal life by grace not by works, and who removes all fear and gives peace.

Under the cover of darkness, we went back to the village that night and provided a copy of God's Book to one of the youth. The next morning, I awoke to take one more walk on the beach before departing for Huế. As I did, I was surrounded by children and youth wanting to talk with me. We walked and talked and laughed and played. Most of them dispersed as we came closer to the hotel except for one girl in her late teens. She came close to me and in a soft voice said, "Can I have something from America?" I replied, "I'm sorry but I don't have anything with me to give you." She looked around to see if anyone was watching, got a little closer and whispered, "Can I have a Bible?" She shared that she and her friends read from the one we provided the night before. She really liked it and wanted one of her own. I was pleased to oblige. As we left for Huế, I remembered yet again the words of the Lord from Isaiah 55:11 that had been an inspiration many times in my life: *"My words will not return empty, without accomplishing what I desire …"*

Huế City became my favorite city in the world on my first day there, and it remains so today. The cultural, historical and educational center of Vietnam is surrounded by UNESCO World Heritage historical sites and the most congenial people. It is situated on the Perfume River, named such because of flowers from orchards upriver that fall into the water in autumn, giving the river a perfume-like aroma. The Citadel, the former Imperial City of Vietnam, is there. Dragon boats and sampans traverse up and down the river. Cyclos, three-wheeled bicycles called rickshaws in other countries, serve as pedicabs. Shops selling and making clothes line Phạm Ngũ Lão Street. The pristine Thuan An beach is less than 30 minutes away and has small hamlets of fishermen who have handed down their trade for generations. A walk beside the river in the morning will bring numerous invitations from strangers to sit, sip coffee, and talk about family.

I became close to Ben, my roommate on the trip, and Jim, our team leader. Ben was a former chopper pilot in the war and had visited Huế before. On our first evening, Ben invited me to join him to see the Water Puppet show, a popular tourist attraction in Huế. On the way there, walking parallel to the river on Lê Lợi Street, we passed a tiny dwelling. The father was sitting with his son beside a small display cabinet with candies, crackers and small cans of Coke. We had just eaten and didn't need anything, but I asked Ben if we could stop and buy something to bless the family.

The home was no more than eight or nine feet wide and fifteen feet deep. Two light bulbs rigged from the street pole hung inside. They had a small cabinet for clothes and a couple of shelves with pots and plates. There was no running water that we could see. A bamboo mat on a frame was covered with mosquito netting for a bed. Here lived a father, a mother, a teenage son completely crippled by childhood illness and unable to care for himself, an adorable 11-year-old daughter, and another toddler, a girl. They were poor, terribly poor by the standards with which we judge. Yet they were so rich in their joy, their love for one another, and their hospitality.

I was impressed by this family. Ben and I sat with the father and son as Ben communicated with the little Vietnamese he remembered. Eventually the 11-year-old daughter (whose name means "happiness" in Vietnamese) and the mother, came home. We arranged to come back to their home a couple of days later.

When we arrived back at their home, the entire family was waiting with two friends of the father and a translator. The translator was a taxi driver who was veteran of the "American War." He and Ben had a wonderful time together. Lidia had sent some women's and girl's clothing for me to give to a family in Vietnam. I was pleased to give the clothes to this family. We also brought some basic medication and a copy of the eternal Book (the Bible) hidden neatly into a granola bar box.

We had a lovely time with the family. We visited for hours. The 11-year-old daughter showed me some of her schoolwork and pictures she had drawn. I raved over them. We had tea and snacks and enjoyed one another, with one brief interruption when some police walked down the street. We immediately became tourists about to buy some soda and crackers until they passed by.

Later that evening, I pulled out the granola bar box and removed the Vietnamese Bible. In a circle that hid The Book, I talked about the Living God and shared from various passages of scripture. Matthew 6:33-34 touched the mother deeply. I had her read the words, *"So don't worry about what you shall eat or drink, or wear, or where you shall live. Your Heavenly Father knows that you need these things."* She clutched the Bible in her hands and drew it close to her heart with tears in her eyes. Tears were also in the eyes of the translator as he shared our words with the family. The Lord was speaking to his heart as well.

I gave the family my address and one of my business cards. A couple of months after arriving home, I received a letter from the 11-year-old daughter. I had some friends translate it for me. I wrote a return letter which my friends translated and sent it to her. A couple of months later, I received another note. This went on for years, until the letters stopped. I did not hear from the family for a while. Then one day, an email popped up in my inbox. It was the older daughter! She had kept my business card with my email address and, now in college, was able to email me.

I returned to Huế 14 years after my first visit. I had prayed for the family all those years. The reunion was wonderful. God had blessed them with a better home. We spent several days together. I asked if they still had the Bible I had given them years before. The older daughter turned to a bookshelf and pulled it out. Much of our time after that was spent sharing the story of God.

On my final day there, after sharing the hope and new life that can be found in Jesus, the daughter's eyes lit up as she said, "I want this! I want it!" I asked her if she would like to pray and open her heart to Christ as her Savior. She said, "Yes, if you help me pray. I have never prayed to God before." And so, I did.

As soon as we finished praying, I began to doubt. "Maybe she doesn't mean it. Maybe she's only doing this because she respects me." As soon as I had those thoughts, she said, "Mr. Tom, I now understand that all this time it has not been you who loved us, but Jesus who loved us through you!" Only the Holy Spirit could reveal that truth to her.

My next trip to Huế was with my family several years later. On our first day, we learned that the younger daughter and younger brother had read the Bible and believed in God. The younger daughter shared her beautiful story with us: *"We were too poor when you met us, Mr. Tom. My parents could not buy us magazines and comic books like the other children had. But you gave us Bible stories in our language. My brother and I read them over and over again. That is how God showed us that He is real and we began to believe in Him. I now realize that it was because of our poverty that God had the opportunity to show us His love!"*

The oldest daughter, the first to believe, became like a daughter to us. Her sister is very close to us as well. Along with their brother, they continue to believe in God and His Great Book. The oldest daughter is now married, and her son is our godson. Their family is like our second family. All of this has happened because we listened to a little whisper that said, "Buy some crackers and a Coke from that man to bless his family." I'm so glad we did.

After that initial visit to Huế in 1996, we departed the city and headed north to Đông Hà. We secured an additional government guide and proceeded to visit Bru Montagnard villages at Khe Sanh and near the border of Laos. An additional guide was required in these restricted areas. A man named Anh had been our guide from the beginning of the trip, appointed by the government with a driver to care for our team but more importantly for them, to watch our activity. Anh was a gentleman, very taken by the camaraderie of our group and the presence of something greater. Our new guide was not as congenial.

The Bru are indigenous peoples from the Central Highlands in Vietnam. They call themselves *Degar*. The French gave them the name *Montagnard* which means "mountain people." Some Vietnamese call them *Moi*, or "savages." Montagnard tribesmen fought valiantly beside American special forces during the war. They still pay for that today.

They are extremely poor and plagued with sickness and disease. At the time of our visit, the infant mortality rate was 40 percent, with four of every ten children dying of treatable diseases, like malaria and dysentery. The lack of medical supplies and health care made medical treatment impossible.

We took Highway 16 from Đông Hà along the old DMZ and stopped at a Bru village by the border of Laos. Our team leader, Jim, had visited this village a couple years before. While his team was distributing medical supplies and instructions were translated from English to Vietnamese to Bru, Jim snuck away from the team and placed bibles in the Bru language in their humble huts. Returning a year later, he found that the entire village had received Christ as Savior. Without a teacher, missionary, or any other access to the outside world, they read the bible by faith and the Holy Spirit taught them. Not only had they become Christians, but they had shared the story of God with some neighboring tribes who received the hope of the Gospel as well. The bible and its Author were enough to bring this miracle.

Jim, Ben and I snuck away from the group and found a hut with the words "Jesus Lord" and a cross painted on the side. The pastor came and met us. While we spoke with him, a messenger from a Bru village in Laos came and said repeatedly, "Beaucoup bibles! Beaucoup bibles!" They needed more bibles. They received some more that day. In order not to raise suspicion, our time with them was short.

Our new guide was not happy with us. He made it clear he hated Americans and ridiculed us at every opportunity, much to his pleasure. Our other guide, Anh, was noticeably quiet in the village. His eyes focused on me so much that Jim and Ben approached me and recommended my extreme caution. We did not know why, but Anh's attention was trained on me.

We finished distributing the medical supplies and said goodbye to the villagers. While loading the minibus, Anh approached me. He made a figure of a halo over his head with his finger and said, "You have an aura of light over you like a holy man." From that moment to the end of the trip, Anh treated me with great respect. He carried my luggage, sat me in the front seat of the tour bus that he had previously occupied, assisted me looking for souvenirs and ordered food for me in restaurants. I do not know what he saw, but it opened the door to share openly with him about God, a message he was hungry and open to hear. I have not heard from Anh since we said goodbye, but my prayers for him have continued. I know the seed will not return empty.

From there, we visited the Khe Sanh battlefield, walking carefully because of live ordinance still littering the area. We saw many unexploded grenades and explosives that had been unearthed by farmers and set in a pile on the side of the field. Arriving at the second Bru Village, the chief came to us and asked us to pray for his brother-in-law. He had hit a live shell while working his vegetable garden. It exploded, breaking his leg and lacerating his leg and body. Infection had set into the bone in the two weeks since the injury. A doctor on our team examined him and saw the obvious, that he needed immediate medical attention. The leg needed to be opened, the bone reset, and the bone scraped for infection, all impossibilities in this remote area.

The chief said, "We have prayed to our gods, but they have not heard us. We know that you are holy men. Perhaps if you pray to your God, He will hear and heal my brother-in-law."

Ben looked at Jim and me and quoted the words of Peter in Acts 3:6, *"I don't have any silver or gold for you. But I'll give you what*

I have. In the name of Jesus Christ ... walk!" Knowing God had us there for a reason and knowing if God didn't heal the man he could die, the three of us joined together and prayed discreetly for him.

Our prayer was not as discreet as we would have liked. The second guide saw us and began to mock us, laughing at our faith and prayers. "There is no God! You stupid Americans pray to nothing!" That was fine. We know the God we serve, and we left the rest in His hands.

Upon returning home, I still had a mission. I contacted Bruce and gave him a report of the trip. He was thrilled. Just like I had done for him, he prayed for me every day while I was in Vietnam.

Bruce was still putting his life back together. Many obstacles still stood in the way. Drugs nearly destroyed his life after the war. Putting the pieces back together was a painstaking process.

A couple of weeks after arriving home from Vietnam, the ministry of Vietnam veterans with which I was connected sent me a beautiful appreciation gift. It was a one- foot-tall Fallen Soldier statue with boots, rifle and helmet titled, "My Hero." I opened it up, admired it, showed it to Lidia, and said to her, "You know what I have to do with this." She nodded her head yes.

I took a small piece of paper and wrote, "To my hero." I put the paper inside, taped up the box and mailed it to Bruce.

We had an evening meal and staff meeting at our house a few days later. The phone rang about 7:30 pm. It was Bruce.

"Hello Tom. It's Bruce."

"Bruce," I replied, "How are you?"

Bruce burst into tears, weeping bitterly and completely unable to compose himself. He wept loudly for several minutes. I knew nothing to do but to pray for him. When he composed himself enough to speak, he said, "Tom, you saved my life today."

Bruce had reached the end of his road. His family and life had fallen completely apart. Leaving work that day, he told God it was over. He would end his life that night.

He came home and found a box on the steps of his mobile home. He opened it up and found the words, "To my hero." In God's divine providence, the gift was delivered the day Bruce needed it most.

Everything changed from that moment forward. Bruce got his life together, and by God's grace, he became a minister and chaplain for drug addicts and alcoholics. Bruce joined us for outreach on the very streets of Detroit where he once bought and used drugs. He even met a lady with whom he shared drugs decades before and saw that her life had been changed by God's grace. Bruce died the next year, but his life was renewed, because God never forgets.

I have a dear friend, Roger Helle, who is one of my heroes. Roger is a Vietnam veteran and one of my prayer partners. Less than a year after I was in Vietnam, Roger made another journey back with Jim and Ben. They took a similar trek as we did in 1996. In Đông Hà, they picked up an additional government guide. By God's divine providence, it was the same one who hated Americans and mocked us when we prayed. When he saw Jim and Ben, he recognized them from the year before and said, "I saw a miracle! I saw a miracle!" Roger shares the story in his book *A Time to Kill: A Time to Heal:*

"We did not quite understand what he was trying to say. When we got to the village, there was a flurry of activity, which is normal. Soon, the village chief appeared and grabbed Jim. He yelled something out and several kids ran off. Soon, the crowd around us parted and a man walked to us. Jim about fell over. He looked at us and said, "This is the chief's brother-in-law I told you about!" I looked at this man standing before us, beaming… Now the new guide was standing by us, pointing to the man and saying, "See, see, I saw a miracle!"

"The guide who had been with the team (the year before) was bringing a tour group of Germans to see the village. This happened several months after the (1996) team's visit. As they drove to the village, the guide told them about the man who was killed when he hit a grenade while hoeing a garden.

"When he arrived at the village and saw the man healed, God touched his heart, and he made a commitment to Christ. Jim had given him a New Testament as a gift the year before, and he prayed the prayer in the back to give his heart to Christ."[1]

As a result of that miracle, many Bru Montagnards believed in God. The news of this miracle and of the conversion of these Bru people became a testimony that was heard in many places in the nation. The God of the bibles smuggled into that village became the God of Bru villages across Vietnam. Yet again God showed us that His Word will not return without accomplishing what He desires and fulfilling His purposes (Isaiah 55:11).

I was finally able to return to that village 23 years after my first visit. As I walked into the village with some Vietnamese friends, the people quickly ran into their huts. I can only imagine what they thought seeing this 6'2" American coming into their village. Only curious children remained outside. I began to give candy to the children. My assistant distributed some balls and toys and began playing with them. Little by little, the parents came out of their huts.

I had scanned pictures from my 1996 visit to their village and loaded them in my phone to show the people. They were amazed at the pictures, commenting, "That's my sister! . . . That's my nephew! . . . That's my aunt!" Then they saw a picture of a man in a faded, red shirt. They began speaking with excitement. A young man ran from the group to a hut in the distance. A few moments later, he emerged with the man who was in the picture 23 years before. The man remembered the visit of our team.

My presence with them was accepted. I spoke with the people, sharing how I had never forgotten them and how I had prayed to the Living God for them for 23 years. God began a new connection in that village. I promised them that I would come back.

As we were leaving, a young man who spoke a little English walked with me to our vehicle. He said, "You not come back. No one come back. Everyone forget us." His words struck me to the core of my being. I promised him that I would come back, and I did, five days later.

We brought clothing for the children and various hygiene supplies for the families. I also brought words from The Book. I shared about the Living God, the God who made the land and the trees, the rivers and the rice fields. He also made each one of them and said in His Great Book that He knew them before they were born and ordained a purpose, a destiny, for each of their lives (Jeremiah 1:5). Their hearts were open to hear and receive.

The situation with the Montagnards has not changed much in 23 years. Malaria, dysentery, tuberculosis, Dengue fever, typhoid and other diseases are commonplace. Children are under-sized and often sickly because of malnutrition. Gastrointestinal and dermatological diseases are prevalent because of contaminated river water. Literacy levels are quite low.

One thing was different from my first visit. There was no witness of Christ. The powers that be had most likely eradicated that many years before.

My next visit to the village was ten months later. Management and staff at a hotel that we frequent gave us large quantities of clothing for children and adults. It was a pleasure to see how appreciative and respectful the people were to receive it. We installed five water purification filters. Each one will provide up to 170 gallons of purified water each day. We have since installed 15 more. We want to make purified water accessible to each family. We want to make Living Water accessible to them, too.

I have become close to the young man who thought we would never return. On my last visit, he introduced me to his family and asked for a picture with his family and me. He took my arm and placed it in his arm, rubbing my arm affectionately. God has a plan for his life and family.

The people need hope in tangible forms. We are implementing a strategic plan to improve the quality of life of these beautiful people through medical treatment and medical education. We have translated a village health manual that will support education in hygiene, dental hygiene, pre-natal care, post-natal care, nutrition, first aid and other relevant topics. We are providing water purification filters and children's vitamins. We are also seeking to enhance literacy among children and youth. We are working with a growing network of American and Vietnamese businessmen, educators and medical professionals that God has miraculously placed together. God is being glorified as people are becoming aware of the Living God and the hope that can be found in His Son, Jesus.

What David Wilkerson said to me in those early years in the Bronx is true for all of us: "Jump in the deep end." My translation - *Don't stay planted where you are. Launch. Trust. Jump. Jesus will catch you and lead you into the plans He designed just for you.*

Jesus *"had to go through Samaria"* (John 4:4). Through an earthly perspective, it didn't make sense for Jesus to go through Samaria. It was not acceptable for Him to go through Samaria. No good Jew went through Samaria! But in a heavenly perspective, there was a wounded, forsaken woman by a well that would hear these life-changing words from the mouth of Jesus, *"I am the Messiah!"* (John 4:26). Sometimes it doesn't make sense in an earthly perspective that God would send us "there," but in a heavenly perspective, God knew before we were born that He would send us there.

If what we choose to do is within our talents, giftings and skill sets, why do we need God? It is when He stretches us beyond our capacities that we see His hand at work and His glory revealed.

As for me, it is my desire to go wherever God wants me to go, especially to the suffering and those who have never heard, and to do whatever God wants me to do. He has never failed me. I know He never will. By His grace, I will follow.

The words in Hebrews 13:8 are as true today as they were when they were written: *"Jesus is the same yesterday, today and forever."* He is able to do today everything we read about in the Bible. He *never* changes. He is *always* faithful. His love is *unconditional* and *unfailing.* His grace and mercy are *never ending.*

"No eye has seen, no ear has heard, no mind has imagined what God has in store for those who love Him" (1 Corinthians 2:9).

---

[1] *A Time to Kill: A Time to Heal,* Roger Helle. Derek Press, 2007.

Conclusion

Send Me

"Here I am. Send me."

Isaiah 6:8

The invitation to walk with Jesus remains as present as ever before. I know that God has laid out my footsteps to bring His hope, His unconditional love, and His peace to those who do not know and have not heard. His faithful presence has never failed us. He provided when there was absolutely no other way. He moved our mountains or taught us to climb. Teaching us to climb always taught us more about Him. His grace guided us when we leapt by faith and lovingly caught us when we slipped along the way.

There have been many lessons that He has taught us in this journey.

Human skill, knowledge and understanding cannot make an eternal difference in this world. That which we need the most is the favor and presence of God. With those two unmerited blessings, any challenge can be faced, any obstacle overcome, and the miracles of His hands will be seen working among the people.

Authentic church is not necessarily expressed in the ways that we define it. One of my mentors, Floyd McClung Jr., defined church in the words of Jesus: *"Where two or three are gathered in My name, I am there"* (Matthew 18:20). It is in living that scripture that we have seen His hand of mercy and experienced His presence the most. Floyd once told me that one of the easiest places to hide from God is in a dead church. How true. I would rather worship God under a tree or in the courtyard of the projects with two or three than inside the walls of a church that stirs my emotions but does not rend my soul and radically challenge me to serve a dying world.

We are not consumed by His glory. We are consumed with ourselves, and the result of our defection from His priorities is seen in the lost world around us searching for answers that we have but fail to tell. Only brokenness and repentance can bring us back.

Victim mentality keeps countless people in bondage. In truth, there has only been one victim who has ever walked the face of the earth. That is the innocent One, Jesus, who, without blemish or sin, took the failures, woundedness, filth and deception of all people and nailed it to the cross. As long as we consider ourselves victims, the full power of His redeeming touch cannot be felt. Yes, we must come to Him even in the surrender of our feelings of victimization or we will never be healed.

The church has been given a great commission, a "go-mission," to reveal His truth and the beauty of His love to the nations. Whether we have succeeded or failed in this endeavor is for God alone to judge, but our focus on self-improvement, self-sufficiency, self-preservation and self-affirmation using (and abusing) the truth entrusted to us has deterred us from our heavenly call. We must return to that which is most important to the heart of Almighty God: the salvation of souls. Jesus Christ said that He came to *"seek and to save those who are lost"* (Luke 19:10). Our purpose is the same. This will take a realignment of our priorities and a grafting into our hearts of the passion of the Almighty for the lost. If we allow that to happen, it will change us as we go forth to change the world.

I often wonder if we are not like the people of God during the writing of Haggai the prophet. They took the materials that were intended to be used for the building of God's temple and instead built unto themselves. Do we recognize the parallel? Have we not taken the abilities, talents, and knowledge that God has given us to build His Kingdom and used them to build our own kingdoms for our own glory? The same call of repentance through Haggai is the same we must hear today, to return to God and to complete the tasks He has given us, *"that I [God] may be pleased with it and be glorified..."* (Haggai 1:8).

A miracle that God performed in my wife's family has inspired and guided me since I heard it many years ago. While living under the socialist government in Chile, basic necessities were hard to come by. Long lines formed at grocery stores that were virtually empty. Hardship became common place in what had been one of the most stable democracies and economies of South America.

One of the things that was scarce was cooking oil, a basic commodity that you don't miss until you do not have it. My father-in-law was able to purchase a large barrel of cooking oil. They immediately began to share the oil with family, friends, and church members. My mother-in-law shared that a worker walked by her kitchen window and saw her cooking with oil. He stated that they hadn't had any in his house for weeks, so she shared some oil with him.

Very quickly, the oil was nearly depleted. Having placed a deposit on the barrel, my father-in-law measured what remained with a measuring stick and found that about one-and-a-half inches remained in the bottom of the barrel. He asked Lidia's two brothers to empty the remaining oil into jars so that he could return the barrel. Lidia helped as they filled all the jars they had, but oil remained in the barrel.

They took the initiative to bring some pots from the kitchen and began to fill them. After filling a few pots, my brother-in-law Israel looked at my wife and his elder brother and said what was unexplainable without God, "We've poured out all of this oil, but the barrel is heavier than when we started!"

They summoned their father who took the same measuring stick to measure the oil remaining in the barrel. The line was still present on the measuring stick from the previous time. This time, however, after filling numerous pots and jars with oil, there was more than one-and-a-half feet of oil in the barrel. Just as He did for the widow in 2 Kings 4, God multiplied the oil.

They continued to share the oil. That barrel of oil lasted until after the socialist government was overthrown and grocery stores were restocked and opened to the public. My wife and her family have the deep conviction that, if they had not shared the oil as they did, God would have had no reason to multiply it. Because they shared what they had with those in need, God multiplied it back unto them.

We have seen God do the same in our family and ministry since we launched out by faith to the South Bronx. Every step, however difficult, has always been accompanied by enough grace to get us through. God has been very real and very present in every challenge. We have made sure that He is very present in our praise.

I prayed, "God, lead me forth into the paths that You have charted for my life." He did. He invited me to walk with Him down streets where He was already working, already calling people by name. He invited me into a world of desperation, poverty and pain. He invited me into a world of learning to lean hard on Him, following in blind faith and often not knowing what tomorrow might bring. He invited me, along with my family and those He would bring to walk beside Him with us, to become His hands, His shoulders, His tears, to reveal His heart with a voice of passionate love and a cry of mercy and grace.

Jesus has so graciously opened my eyes and heart to the revelation that *He has never changed.* He still is the same as He was with Joshua, with David, with Bartimaeus on the roadside. He still gives second chances like He did with Peter. He still stops the hemorrhages of wounded and broken lives like He did with the woman who, in a last-ditch effort, touched the hem of His garment. Jesus is the same *"yesterday, today and forever"* and He will be just that in our lives if we, with simple, mustard-seed faith, allow Him to be the Lord He yearns to be to and through every one of us.

Answering God's call to bring His penetrating light into the darkest places does not come without resistance. As we answered and followed, the battle for souls became more than an inspiring expression. It became our journey. We endured cold winters without heat in a rat-infested building. We endured death threats, rejection, assault, disappointments, death, and cancer. We raised our children amid economic, spiritual, and moral poverty. We suffered the tragic loss of those too young to be taken from this earth. We encountered opposition and rejection. We poured out His love in the context of violence, oppression, and moral deprivation. We fought hard for people to be freed from the chains that had bound them in darkness for years and even generations. We experienced His glory and we have seen Him prove His Word, His love, His grace ... *HIMSELF* . . . over and over and over.

There were many nay-sayers along our journey. People who brought words of discouragement and said it couldn't be done. They said, "You can't start a ministry in the South Bronx. It's too dangerous for you and especially for your family." They said, "Detroit is too divided. White and black will never unite together in ministry." They said, "You can't take a ministry team to Cuba ... You can't go inside those favelas in Sao Paolo ... You can't go to that closed nation with the Gospel ..."

The nay-sayers were wrong not because of me, but because of the God I serve. They were wrong because I did not initiate any of this. God planned it while I was in my mother's womb. They were wrong because Jesus said, *"I have been given all authority in heaven and on earth. Therefore, go ..."* and then He said, *"I am with you always"*(Matthew 28:19-20).

They were right about this: I couldn't do it. Not at all. Nobody could. But He could. And He did, because *"nothing is impossible with God"* (Luke 1:37).

Hope must have hands and it must have feet. It must have shoulders to lean on and knees to intercede. It must have tear-stained cheeks from hearts that feel the pain of the people, hastening someone to do something not just tangible but *right* in response, pursuing healing and justice. It must go to the oppressed and rejected, inviting them to come into eternal fellowship with the Healer, Savior, and Lover of their souls.

Salt is not made to put on salt; it's made to put on what has no life. There are plenty of people around us, everywhere, living life without hope, without real joy, without lasting peace, and without the knowledge that they have a unique destiny designed by the Living God in unfathomable, unconditional, everlasting love. They are waiting for us to not just tell them, but to *show them* that Jesus is alive.

Leaving a church on a recent mission, I was reminded of Isaiah's call. As I sat pondering Isaiah 6:8, I began quoting the passage to myself that I had memorized decades ago. The words struck me personally as they always have: *"Whom shall I send? Who will go for us?"*

With a fishing village on the left and rice patties on the right, I began to respond as Isaiah did, *"Here I am,"* but I could speak no more. It was like the Holy Spirit grabbed my tongue and my thoughts and put the brakes on. He would not let me continue to the final phrase of that verse.

I again attempted several times to finish the verse but could not. Then the thought came to me, I believe from His Spirit: I have become the sent. I no longer need to say, *"Here I am. Send me."* I now say, *"Here I am. I am sent. I am here. Use me now for Your glory and help me complete the work that You ordained for me."*

Walking with Jesus down the streets and alleyways of neglected urban communities, the dirt paths of oppressed villages in closed nations, and every place in between, I found that Jesus knew the people by name. He knew their fears. He knew their wounds. He knew their hopes and their dreams. He heard their cries. He longed to heal them and set them free. He longed for them to know Him by name. He just needed someone to be present with His hope, transforming love and grace.

Jesus wants to walk into the places where hope departed a long time ago. He wants to walk to the doors of the broken and empty wherever they are. He longs to be present where there is desperation, hopelessness, and pain. He calls you and I to walk there with Him.

I have learned something truly spectacular walking with Jesus: when I say yes to follow Him where and how He chooses, wounded, hopeless, and neglected people begin to live again.

Stop and ponder these words one more time: *"Whom shall I send? Who will go for us?"* Hear Jesus say to you, *"Walk with Me."*

Stand and proclaim your answer *"Here I am!"* and become one of the sent. Then you will discover the absolute and unchanging truth of these words:

"Anything is possible if a person believes."
(Mark 9:23)

The Gospel

I have referred to the gospel in this book. The book of Romans in the New Testament begins by presenting the gospel as the "Good News" about Jesus. His mission in life, death, and resurrection was to restore our relationship with the Living God. For those who believe, it fills every day with hope that will overcome every challenge we face. It propels everyone who believes into the unique destiny designed by the Living God while we were still in our mother's wombs. It is life lived to the fullest walking daily with our Savior on this earth, who makes the impossible possible and proves He really is God.

Unfortunately, the gospel has morphed into something more like a cultural presentation of a particular religion in the west. It has become "churched," conveyed to the world through impressive presentations and gifted communicators inside nice buildings who inspire a particular group of people but whose message is increasingly irrelevant. In many places, it has become too disconnected, distracted and inwardly focused to bring radical change to the suffering world around it.

That is not the good news.

I had the privilege of leading the chapel ministry for my son's university hockey team. In our first meeting with 12 of the players, I asked each to share three things about themselves the others did not know. It was an entertaining way to break the ice and get to know each other.

I was the last one to share three things they did not know about me: I have a doctorate in music and once performed for President Ronald Reagan and, on a separate occasion, for Barbara Bush. I have Level 4 coaching certification with USA Hockey. I hate religion and the One whom I serve hates religion, too.

The last statement caused their eyes to open widely in bewilderment as if saying, *"How can someone who has dedicated his life to ministry hate religion?"*

I asked what religion means to them. They responded that religion is a tradition they occasionally participate in, mostly out of respect, but it does not relate to their world. They also shared it has not made a difference in their lives, and they were not driven to pursue it.

My response to them was simple: my Jesus did not suffer and die for that. He did not suffer and die for us to be entertained, motivated by an inspiring speaker, or bored to sleep with irrelevant words that make no impact on our lives.

Nor did He suffer and die so that we can spend our lives trying to be good enough. We can never be good enough.

In Ephesians 2:8-9, Paul the Apostle said, *"God saved you by His grace when you believed. And you can't take credit for this; it is a gift from God. Salvation is not a reward for the good things we have done…"* Not a reward for our works? That's really good news!

Paul continues in verse 10, *"For we are God's masterpiece. He has created us anew in Christ Jesus, so we can do the good things He planned for us long ago."*

That's good news.

Jesus came to this earth with a message that opposes our culture in a multiplicity of ways. His life and teachings challenge us to love our neighbors as ourselves and place the needs of others above our own. He says that the greatest in the kingdom of God is the servant of all. He tells us if someone asks us to walk a mile with him, we should walk two. If he asks for our coat, we should give him our shirt also.

Then He takes us deeper into issues of our hearts. He instructs us to love those who hate us. Forgive those who have injured us. Pray for those who persecute us. Have the same attitude of Jesus who took the form of a servant. Then go and make an eternal difference in this world.

Then Jesus did what no one expected. He took the form of the lowest servant, placed the curse of the sin of the entire world - including yours and mine - on his shoulders, and sacrificed His sinless life as the punishment for our sin. And then, as if that wasn't enough, He took the keys of sin, death and hell from Satan himself and rose from the dead with life for all who believe.

The things that Jesus tells us to do are not possible without divine help, but they are with Jesus in us. They become the fruit of an eternal change from within. This change, rooted in belief in Jesus and a commitment to follow His ways, does not invite us into a Western tradition or a boring religion. It invites us into a heart-change that explodes with joy. It destroys the power of sin and shame and replaces them with peace, hope, overflowing love and life – the greatest life here and the greatest life to come. It invites us to walk with Jesus discovering every day that He is alive, He is relevant, He is patient, He is gentle, He is all-powerful, He is wise, He is Healer, He is Savior, and He is friend, the greatest and most faithful friend we will ever have.

We hear this and wonder, what must we do to receive all of this? The remarkable truth is that we just need to do one thing: believe.

That is really good news.

Lord, for anyone reading this who wants to live life to the fullest and be free of the curse of sin and shame, come to them now. Let them feel Your love embracing them. Wash away the bitter tastes that life can bring. Fill every empty space with all that You are. Become the Lord of their lives. Walk with them down the pathway You have prepared, one of discovery, purpose and eternal joy. Surround them with Your peace. Carry the weight of their troubles. Show them who You are.

"To all who believed Him and accepted Him, He gave the right to become children of God" (John 1:12).

Getting Involved with Urban Harvest Ministries

Perhaps you would like to become involved in Urban Harvest Ministries. There are several ways that you can do that:

Urban Harvest Ministries (UHM) leads strategic outreach and leadership empowerment in New York City through *The Harvest Center* in the South Bronx.

This is the first outreach center established by UHM in 1995. Mission teams from local churches and colleges have the opportunity to serve in various forms of community outreach. These experiences are life changing. Internships are available for college students and young adults to serve and be empowered in urban ministry. Pastors and church leaders can join us for ministry training intensives which combine dialogs on ministry and hands-on outreach.

Hope for the City is a multi-church initiative established in Detroit in 2005. *Hope for the City* focuses on leadership empowerment and strategic

outreach in urban communities and among immigrant peoples. Through this ministry, dozens of churches have been empowered to pastor the streets around them and thousands have heard the gospel. Mission teams and interns are welcome to serve in outreach with *Hope for the City.* Pastor and church leader ministry intensives are also available in Detroit.

The Bridge School of Missions is an extension of the leadership development and empowerment in Great Commission that Urban Harvest Ministries has conducted in many cities and nations. UHM has established *The Bridge* to equip and empower servant leaders in Great Commission ministry. Topics of instruction include servant leadership, sharing our faith, relational discipleship, strategic outreach, worship, empowerment of the poor, sharing our faith, reaching the unchurched, child discipleship and more. *The Bridge* classes are offered via Zoom. A certificate program is available to those interested.

Dr. Grassano frequently visits churches and faith groups, challenging and empowering servant leaders to change their world.

More information for all the above is available by contacting us at urbanharvest@uhm.cc.

Urban Harvest Ministries is a faith-based organization operating solely through the generosity of churches, businesses, and people like you. This partnership is vital to continue outreach and empowerment in cities and nations. To become a *Partner in Ministry* with UHM, go to urbanharvestministries.org or contact us at urbanharvest@uhm.cc.

Follow Urban Harvest Ministries on Facebook, Twitter @UrbanHarvestMin and Instagram @UrbanHarvestMin. Visit our website www.urbanharvestministries.org to learn more about our ministry and to sign up for our newsletter updates.

We ask for your prayers as we continue the mission of reaching the lost, the hurting, and those who have not heard the hope of the Gospel of Jesus Christ.

Thank you!

About the Author

Dr. Tom Grassano is an author, speaker, and change maker who leads strategic outreach to the poor and disenfranchised. He is an accomplished performer and composer with a Doctorate in Music from Florida State University. After serving in summer outreach projects for many years in and outside the U.S., he left his music career and founded *Urban Harvest* in 1994 in the South Bronx community called "Fort Apache." Opposition, limited resources and even death threats did not prevent fulfillment of the vision to bring the hope of the gospel to the wounded and broken.

Dr. Grassano expanded *Urban Harvest* to Detroit in 2005 and founded *Hope for the City*, an initiative uniting people across cultural, racial and economic boundaries to bring hope to suffering communities in Detroit. He is also the founder of *The Bridge School of Missions,* which is equipping emerging leaders to fulfill the Great Commission, and *Go-Mission,* which is empowering the poor, building bridges across cultures and providing life-changing opportunities to serve in the US and abroad.

Tom has dedicated his life to bringing hope to the unreached and disenfranchised and empowering others to do the same. He has served as a speaker, teacher, and outreach leader in more than 40 states and 20 nations. His greatest passion is his family – his wife, Lidia, and his children, Angel and Tommy. United in mission, God is using this family as agents of hope and catalysts for change in some of the most desperate places.

You will find more information on Dr. Grassano, including his blog, at www.tomgrassano.com.